REVOLUTION IN ROME

To Jane

REVOLUTION IN ROME

DAVID F. WELLS

Associate Professor of Church History and the
History of Christian Thought at Trinity Evangelical
Divinity School, Deerfield, Illinois

TYNDALE PRESS
39 BEDFORD SQUARE, LONDON WC1B 3EY

Copyright © by the Inter-Varsity Christian Fellowship
of the United States of America
First British edition February 1973
ISBN 0 85111 310 9

Printed and bound in Great Britain by
Hazell Watson and Viney Ltd, Aylesbury, Bucks

CONTENTS

FOREWORD

For over 400 years Protestants and Roman Catholics have remained in the entrenched positions into which they dug themselves at the Reformation. Just about their only contact has been to lob theological grenades at one another across a deserted no-man's land. The argument was largely restricted to the terms of the Reformation Confessions and the Decrees of the Council of Trent. The polemics on both sides have been rigid and often harsh.

Those days are now over. For Rome has changed and is continuing to change, despite her claim to changelessness. As Vatican II asserted: 'Christ summons the Church, as she goes her pilgrim way, to that continued reformation of which she always has need' in so far as she has 'deficiencies in conduct, in Church discipline, or even in the formulation of doctrine' (*Decree on Ecumenism*, para. 6).

Those who blink their eyes in astonishment or shake their heads with incredulity that there could ever be change in a changeless church should study *Revolution in Rome* by my good friend, David Wells. I myself have read it with much pleasure and profit, and would mention the following as some of its chief merits.

First, Dr Wells does his utmost to reach an impartial understanding of the contemporary movements in the Roman Catholic Church. Turning aside from all prejudice, he allows the documents of Vatican II to speak both for themselves and as they are being interpreted by progressive leaders of the 'New Catholicism'. His own comments are scrupulously fair and biblically judicious. In all this he sets an admirable example. Whether we wish to debate or witness or both, we are under an obligation first to listen in order to understand. To decline to do so is to be alike discourteous and ineffective.

Secondly, Dr Wells shows himself very sensitive to the acutely painful personal dilemma in which many contemporary Catholics find themselves. The Roman monolith, which for centuries has appeared inviolable, has at last cracked open. Conservatives and progressives, traditionalists and radicals, are engaged in a fierce power struggle. Because the issues were still open during Vatican II the Council endorsed opinions which oppose, contradict and exclude each other. To many observers the whole church seems to be in unprecedented disarray. Moreover, it is by no means clear whether the final outcome will be the triumph of biblical truth or a disastrous lapse into some kind of existential subjectivism. All Christian people should be praying for those who are caught willy-nilly in this transitional agony, and also that God's Word may 'run and be glorified'.

Thirdly, the book ends with an appeal to the reader to 'speak the truth in love'. In this too Dr Wells has set a fine example. For he has avoided all unnecessary controversy and all bitterness of spirit or expression. He is quite clear, on the one hand, that 'biblical truth cannot be watered down'. He is equally clear, on the other, that 'Christian character must not be violated'. The Protestant churches are committed, so far as they are able, to defend, establish and commend biblical faith. Yet this gives no possible excuse for breaches of Christian charity. We all need to beware lest we hinder a delicate work of the Holy Spirit by our own insensitive clumsiness.

I believe that a careful perusal of this excellent book will lead many into new and more perceptive modes of dialogue and witness. I pray that it may be so.

JOHN STOTT

PREFACE

It is not easy for a Protestant to write a book on Catholics. Too many of these studies have already been written. The route is now so well trodden, the outcome so predictable, that one more addition to this vast literature is likely either to pass unnoticed or at best to excite nothing more than a disinterested yawn. Most authors would agree, I am sure, that outrage would be infinitely preferable to a yawn.

I doubt, however, whether anyone will be outraged by this book (and I hope, perhaps naïvely, that the yawners will be an insignificant minority). But there may be some who will feel uneasy about it. They might fear that too much has been conceded to Rome, for they will search in vain for those warnings about blasphemies and antichrists which used to litter the pages of Protestant works in the past. The fact of the matter is that I have studiously avoided being controversial. This is not, I hope, an indication of weakness or of muddy thinking on my part. It means that in my opinion the new situation will best be explored if we approach it unhampered by the controversial attitudes of the past.

It has been my aim, therefore, to write for both Protestants and Catholics, hoping to appraise both and offend neither. I have sought to be informative without ceasing to be analytical, to be biblical without failing to be charitable. Clarity of mind and generosity of spirit have been my goals. This study may fall short of its stated objectives but lower aims would not have produced a better book.

It may seem strange that a Protestant should undertake a task as formidable as this and one at which even the angels might balk. Would it not be wiser to allow Roman Catholics to analyse themselves? In many instances it probably would.

Those within this tradition have an intuitive grasp of the subject which often eludes the Protestant outsider. At the same time, however, a Protestant can bring to bear on the subject a wealth of knowledge which is largely inaccessible to a Catholic.

This knowledge which the contemporary Protestant has is the product of an historical accident. Present-day Catholicism, on its progressive side, is teaching many of the ideas which the liberal Protestants espoused in the last century. Though progressive Catholics are largely unaware of their liberal Protestant stepbrothers, the family resemblance is nevertheless there. Since these ideas have only come into vogue in Catholicism in the last two decades, they appear brilliantly fresh and innovative. To a Protestant, whether he approves or disapproves of them, they are old hat. The Protestant's greater acquaintance with these ideas and his longer reflection on them can give him an edge in analysing contemporary Catholic thought. Had I not believed this to be the case, I would have joined the angels in balking at such a project.

One of the most frustrating difficulties which I have encountered concerns the matter of sources. Who speaks for Rome today? Who, then, should I read to build up a composite picture of what Catholics now believe? In 1964, Herbert Carson, in his study entitled *Roman Catholicism Today*, answered this question by referring to the theology of the sixteenth-century Council of Trent. The fathers of this council, he said, should be considered the authoritative spokesman for contemporary belief. This left Carson with a relatively uncomplicated task, for the Tridentine fathers are both clear and blunt in their statements. This approach, we may note, was adequate for an assessment of Catholicism as popularly practised then. It did not reflect, however, what was taking place amongst the theologians and intellectuals. For thirty years they had been insisting that their faith could not be equated with what Trent had said, and the church as a whole has now conceded this. Our approach therefore cannot be what Carson's was.

When Catholics themselves are consulted on this problem,

several different answers are given. Some maintain that the teaching of Pope Paul VI is representative of what Catholics believe since he is the head of their Church. That he is the head of the Roman Church is indisputable, but whether he speaks for a majority in the Church is another matter. It is of interest to note that in one recent survey 91% of those priests questioned admitted that they did not feel contraception was either unlawful or sinful as Pope Paul had taught. Proponents of traditional faith, it should also be remembered, were consistently outvoted at the Second Vatican Council. This was a surprise to them no less than to their progressive opponents.

If the conservatives are unrepresentative of what a majority in the Church believes, then we are forced to turn to progressive spokesmen. But which kind of progressive represents the broadest consensus in Catholic thinking? Are we to see in the American secular theologians like Daniel Callahan and Leslie Dewart tomorrow's leaders? And what kind of following do the European radicals have? How are we to view Hans Küng, the rebel from Tübingen University, or Edward Schillebeeckx, the theological leader of the nonconforming Dutch? Perhaps it will be agreed that these theologians go too far. But might the same not be said even of the more moderate European theologians? In this category would be placed the luminaries of French theology, Jean Daniélou, Yves Congar and Louis Bouyer, as well as the most learned and prolific of the German scholars, Karl Rahner. And what are we to make of earlier progressives, like the French philosopher Jacques Maritain, who were regarded as the epitome of radicalism in the 1950s but are now strangely *passé*?

Having pondered this problem for some time, I decided to go back to the documents of the Second Vatican Council, held between 1962 and 1965, and to use these as a base for this study. At least this Council, which spoke for the whole Church, cannot be discounted as unimportant or unrepresentative. In the years since the Council, however, much has taken place in Catholic thought, some modifying and some extending

conciliar teaching. Consequently, Vatican II needs to be
updated. So once again the problem of sources comes into play.
Who should be allowed to update it?

I have allowed progressives rather than conservatives to
state contemporary belief, but even this decision has not
answered the problem completely, for it is not yet clear which
kind of progressive theology will finally emerge as dominant in
Catholic teaching. Who will be the Moses of the New Catholicism? Michael Novak or Hans Küng, Karl Rahner or Jacques
Maritain?

The question, of course, is impossible to answer without
making some pretensions after omniscience. Not since the time
of Hegel has anyone pretended to be omniscient, and I am
reticent to break this tradition. Besides, who would be so brash
as to argue that one man's thought or even the ideas of one
small party could control so massive and all-encompassing a
synthesis as Roman Catholicism? Consequently, the best
solution, it seemed to me, was to accept only those assumptions
which are common to most progressives. In this way, we are
able to utilize a consensus which is broader than any one party
or individual thinker. But does such a consensus exist? To
some, at least, this suggestion is frankly preposterous. It invites
the retort either that I have overlooked the subtle nuances that
distinguish progressive theologians from each other or that I am
simply ignorant of the subject on which I have chosen to write.

That there are important differences and areas of disagree-
ment between progressive Catholic theologians is plain to all.
But this does not mean that there are no assumptions which
they all share. It is the differences which are usually played
up but it is the agreements, I contend, which will ultimately
be important. Consequently, I have made reference to contemporary Catholic theologians as a means of exposing the ideas
which make progressive theology what it is. By seeking the
widest agreement between these theologians, I hope I have
escaped the charge of having depended on unrepresentative or
unimportant theologians.

Another problem which has posed difficulties for me has
been the division of the material. Since Catholicism is in a
state of flux right now, it is more important to see the general
direction in which it is moving than to acquire a storehouse of
knowledge on each individual doctrine. True, the direction is
the cumulative product of the reworking of each doctrine; so
these details cannot be ignored. But it is all too easy to become
lost in the thicket of current debate and fail to see where it is
all leading. Unlike many of my predecessors, then, I have
opted to deal with the subject in broad themes rather than in
detailed doctrine. The thematic approach, however, does have
its drawbacks. It has not been possible, for example, to make
mention of the extraordinary developments taking place in the
Mass and liturgy under any of my topical divisions. This *lacuna*
is an important one but short of adding two appendices to the
book there seemed to be no way in which I could discuss these
developments.

In general, however, it may be said that the differences
between Protestants and Catholics have been lessened as far as
some aspects of the Mass and the liturgy are concerned. The
liturgical movement reaches back into the nineteenth century,
but it was Pius XII's encyclical *Mediator Dei* which gave it new
impetus. The encyclical endorsed the idea of an active partici-
pation of the laity in the worship of the Church. Formerly,
worship had tended to be mechanical, external, carried on by
a priest who was almost oblivious to the people in the Church.
They tended to be merely spectators at an event essentially
external to them. *Mediator Dei* sought to reverse this, arguing
that the faithful are not 'mute onlookers' but should share in
the worship service with the priest. The encyclical even allowed
that the laity has a priestly function to fulfil. While falling
short of endorsing a full doctrine of the priesthood of all
believers, the encyclical went a long way to reversing a
suffocating clericalism under which Catholicism has suffered
and to endorsing the need for subjective involvement in
Christian faith. No longer is Christianity merely a set of

teachings to which the faithful must nod agreement rather like the characters in a Humean dialogue.

Consonant with this development, a new approach to the Mass has emerged. Formerly, the faithful merely enjoyed the celebration from a respectable distance. Now they are intimately involved in it. Indeed, the Mass is often seen as the occasion when they sacrifice themselves to God rather than, as before, when Christ is resacrificed to God. The new concern is no longer with the automatic transformation of the elements into the actual body and blood of Christ (*ex opere operato*) but with the subjective disposition of the participants in the celebration (*ex opere operantis*). The old teaching is not denied; it has merely been pushed into the background. The concern for subjective reality is today evident throughout Catholicism and other manifestations of it are dealt with in the pages which follow.

I have tried to arrange my material, not as a Protestant would do it, but in a form which most nearly corresponds to the way in which Catholics are now thinking. It is customary in some Protestant volumes to see an assessment made of Catholic thought in terms of its importance to the Protestant. What are the origin, nature and consequences of sin? What is the significance of Christ's atonement? How does the sinner appropriate Christ's saving work? How have the doctrines of Catholicism obscured this truth? On what biblical grounds should its teaching on saints, sacraments, Mary, the Pope, tradition and the magisterium be denied? These are important questions, but it was not my purpose to answer them in precisely this form. A Protestant, therefore, may be a little disconcerted in reading over the table of contents to find that none of the questions which are really important to him have apparently been answered. If he will pursue the matter a little further, however, I think he will find that these questions have been answered, in both the text and the footnotes, although not, perhaps, in the form which he might have anticipated.

I have had to cover my subject within the limitations of a

brief book. This has proved frustrating to me and it will not fully satisfy critical readers. All too often it has been impossible either to give supporting evidence for the judgments and conclusions offered or to explain why alternatives have been rejected. Rules have been stated but often without their exceptions. Occasionally I have overgeneralized and over-simplified. No doubt if someone else had written this book, I would have complained about these deficiencies, but I hope my readers are rather more charitable than I am.

After my initial reading, I was able to reflect again on the theology of Vatican II when I taught a course on the New Catholicism with Dr Clark Pinnock. This afforded me a fresh opportunity to test the accuracy of some of these ideas. I also wish to express my gratitude to those who read and criticized the manuscript. These include Dr Murray Harris, Dr Donald Tinder, Dr Geoffrey Bromiley, Dr Eugene Osterhaven and Dr James Hitchcock. Only they will know how great is my debt to them. Although I acknowledge their help, I alone must bear full responsibility for any errors, omissions or misjudgments. Finally, I must express my admiration for the *troika* of typists who managed to decipher my outrageous handwriting. They are Carol Kiehlbach, Carol Langford and Diane Armstrong.

1 THE CHURCH THAT NEVER CHANGES

Catholic apologists in the seventeenth and eighteenth centuries claimed that Rome never changes, and Protestants, for their own reasons, believed them. It was a myth nourished by mutual consent. For Roman Catholics, it was the only defensive posture they felt they could take against the Protestant charge that they had perverted the gospel. How could this be, they retorted, when seventeenth-century Rome believed precisely to the letter what the first-century apostles had believed? The Roman Catholic Church had neither added nor subtracted one iota to or from the biblical teaching. In short, Rome never changes.

Protestants accepted the Catholic claim to support their own contention that Roman theology had always been uniformly bad. It had never changed for the better, but only, perhaps, for the worse. Protestant apologists were quite certain that Rome had perverted the biblical teaching early in her history. Indeed, they said, this defection was so well established in the official pronouncements of the Church that a return to true biblical teaching was impossible. The Reformation had demonstrated this fact. Rome never changes.

The Protestants' point had first been developed in the sixteenth century by the Continental Reformers. At the heart of their Reformation was the belief that Rome had made additions to the gospel, additions which were the product of human tradition.[1] The Reformers argued that where biblical

[1] The Reformers denied that human tradition is revelatory, *i.e.*, that it can augment that revelation contained in Scripture. They did not deny that theologically they stood on the shoulders of earlier theologians like Augustine.

teaching had been filled out in this way, it had also been denied since the theology of the Bible cannot be augmented. Additions to Scripture, such as the Mass, the cluster of ideas which grew up around Mary and the corpus of beliefs that evolved concerning the Pope were all departures from biblical thought. The greater the additions, the more grievous Rome's departures from biblical truth. Consequently, the Reformers argued that the way forward was the way backwards. The layers of tradition by which the gospel had been obscured would have to be rolled back. The theology of the Bible would have to be recovered in its purity if the God of whom it spoke was to be found.[2] This, then, was the polemic which had been established in the sixteenth century and which carried over into the seventeenth and eighteenth centuries.

Within Roman Catholic circles, the Reformation created a profound fear of change. In the centuries which followed, church leaders became nervous about innovation and there emerged a fervent desire to preserve what was left of the Catholic Church. Self-preservation required the Church to establish immediate safeguards against further erosion. These safeguards – a new theological coherence stemming from the Council of Trent and the means of enforcing it, the resuscitated Inquisition – were effective. The Church succeeded in smothering almost every movement which had even a whiff of innovation about it. As the pattern of suppression was established, it produced the hope that the Church would soon

---

Tradition in this latter sense of theological indebtedness is inescapable. Tradition in the sense of revelatory addition is untenable. See F. F. Bruce, *Tradition: Old and New* (Exeter: Paternoster, 1970).

[2] See John Calvin, *Tracts and Treatises*, trans. Henry Beveridge, 3 vols. (Edinburgh: Oliver and Boyd, 1960). In this connection Vol. I, bearing the subtitle 'On the Reformation of the Church' and Vol. III, entitled 'In Defense of the Reformed Faith' are particularly useful. Of value, too, is Martin Luther, *Three Treatises*, trans. Charles Jacobs, A. T. W. Steinhäuser and W. A. Lambert (Philadelphia: Fortress Press, 1960). Luther's treatises were all written in 1520, three years after his historic posting of the theses and the same year in which he was excommunicated. They articulate his reforming ideas with boldness and clarity.

be able to demonstrate beyond any doubt that its teaching – with no exceptions – was an unchanging whole.

Theological innovators have, from the very earliest centuries, skated on thin ice. Rightly or wrongly, novelty and heresy have often been equated. But in the post-Reformation period, Catholics were particularly sensitive on this point and, next to godliness, uniformity became the most desirable virtue. Survival was the prime concern, and Roman Catholics themselves now admit that truth was sometimes the casualty.

Prior to the nineteenth century, then, the embattled Church did not dare to open debate on questions of theological development and change. The Council of Trent had delivered the truth, and nobody was going to tamper with it. It was feared that a few enthusiasts for developing doctrine might easily lead the Church out of the trenches which Trent had dug so effectively. This attitude was well illustrated by Jacques Bossuet, French bishop and perhaps Rome's greatest apologist during the post-Tridentine period in Catholicism. When pressed as to whether Rome's doctrine had ever developed, he conceded that it had – but only geographically. Development in the substance of the Church's teaching, he repudiated; development in the sense of the Church's expanding influence through missionary activity, he accepted. Resolutely turning away from the facts, he claimed that the seventeenth-century Church believed neither more nor less than had the apostles.

By the nineteenth century, the pressure of enforced silence had begun to subside, and some Roman Catholics felt confident enough to climb out of their Tridentine trenches. Bossuet's argument now began to look a little ridiculous. Was it not an ill-formed child of debate, some asked, rather than a candid reflection of what had actually taken place? As a result, beginning with the German theologian John Adam Moehler and the English Cardinal John Henry Newman, an important tactical shift took place. Rome no longer denied that it was teaching matters in the nineteenth century which were not evidently taught by the apostles. The problem was now attacked on a different level altogether. Granting that additions had been made, in what instances were these legitimate?[3]

When the notion of doctrinal addition was accepted in this form, the curtain had begun to drop on the Counter-Reformation. The Reformers' contention was, in one respect at least, being conceded. The massive apologetic structures of the seventeenth and eighteenth centuries were showing signs of decay. Today, a century later, they are in ruins. Vatican II, it might be said, erected a tombstone over this old order and laid the foundation stone for a new one. So completely has Catholic thought emancipated itself from the patterns and apologetic of the past that new theological possibilities are now open to it.

Despite the fact that a violent tremor has passed through Catholic theology in the acceptance of Newman's ideas,[4] some antiquated Protestant seismographs have failed to detect it. As late as 1962, for example, Loraine Boettner wrote:

> The Roman Church has long boasted that she never changes. *Semper Idem* – 'Always the Same' – is her motto. We accept the motto at face value, not that she has not changed or added to the Christian faith which she inherited from the apostolic church, for she certainly has done that, but that the Roman Church has now been frozen into a definite pattern from which she cannot change and which is basically the same today as it was in the days of the Inquisition. What sometimes looks like a change is merely a policy

[3] See Owen Chadwick, *From Bossuet to Newman: The Idea of Doctrinal Development* (London: Cambridge University Press, 1957).

[4] Vatican II accepted and summarized Newman's thought in an important paragraph, the last sentence of which states that 'as the centuries succeed one another, the Church constantly moves forward toward the fullness of divine truth until the words of God reach their complete fulfillment in her' (*Con. Revelation*, 8.) The best translation of the Council documents, from which this sentence is taken, is Walter M. Abbott, ed., *The Documents of Vatican II*, trans. Joseph Gallagher *et al.* (London: Chapman, 1966). See also B. C. Butler's essay entitled 'Newman and the Second Vatican Council', in *The Discovery of Newman: An Oxford Symposium*, ed. John Coulson and A. M. Allchin (London: Sheed and Ward, 1967), pp. 233–246.

of caution which she has been forced to adopt because of public opinion. She changes her methods, but not her spirit.[5]

But the truth is, Boettner notwithstanding, that both the spirit and the doctrine of Catholicism are changing. The Second Vatican Council explicitly said they are changing and one can hardly dismiss such a statement as nothing more than a cunning tactic. The Council affirmed that:

> Christ summons the Church, as she goes her pilgrim way, to the continual reformation of which she always has need, insofar as she is an institution of men here on earth. Therefore, if the influence of events or of the times has led to deficiencies in conduct, in Church discipline, or even in the *formulation of doctrine* [my italics] . . . these should be appropriately rectified at the proper moment.[6]

Consequently, as the Council began, one critic predicted that its work would resemble 'a trial which is taking place in our midst, in which we shall see the Church making frequent admissions of guilt'.[7]

Pope John coined a word to describe the process by which the whole system of Roman Catholic thought was to be probed for deficiency and exposed to redefinition. His word was *aggiornamento*. The full significance of this word rarely carries over into its English translations. Usually it is rendered as *modernization*, which seems to imply that the Council was merely called to give the Church a facelift and perhaps to make its liturgy a little more attractive. The Council was concerned with that, but only peripherally. Something far more radical was intended by John's word.

The Council was called to change the Church's heart no less than its face. To drive home this point, the Council documents

[5] Loraine Boettner, *Roman Catholicism* (London: Banner of Truth, 1966), p. 526.
[6] *Dec. Ecumenism*, 6.
[7] P. Nierman, 'Introduction', *Liturgy in Development* (Glen Rock: Newman Press, 1968), p. viii.

made use of the word *reformatio*, a word which until recently[8]
Protestants have felt they have effectively monopolized
(although this is not entirely the case). Certainly during the
centuries when Catholicism was under siege, the Church
avoided the word like the plague. However, in a move of almost
unparalleled boldness, one which has taken the wind out of
Protestant sails, Vatican II reminded the world that Roman
Catholicism, too, is interested in reformation. To be sure, the
nature of this reformation is quite different from what took
place in the sixteenth century, but it has undeniably opened
new theological vistas.

Contemporary Catholic theologians are now busy exploring
these new possibilities. Vatican II, the American theologian
George H. Tavard has said, 'may mark a passage to a new
theological spirit.'[9] 'A new theology,' Karl Rahner adds,
'must be found which is worthy of Vatican II.' [1] And what will
be the purpose of this activity? Catholic theologians will be
reworking all the staple themes of religious discussion: the
nature of God and man, the meaning of atonement, the
relation of Christian and non-Christian, Church and State,
Christ and culture. So different is the new mentality from the
old and the new theological mandate from the old that Edward
Schillebeeckx likens them to two entirely different worlds.[2]
Gregory Baum has gone even further. In 1968, he replied to
Charles Davis, who had just left the English Church.[3] He
agreed with Davis that traditional Catholicism sometimes

[8] The most significant pre-conciliar study on the problem of reforming the
Church was that of Yves Congar, *Vraie et fausse réforme dans l'Église* (Paris:
Cerf, 1950). The guidelines which he established were enacted in the
Council and later endorsed by Paul VI in his encyclical *Ecclesiam suam*.

[9] George H. Tavard, *The Church Tomorrow* (London: Darton, Longman and
Todd, 1966), p. 25.

[1] Karl Rahner, *The Church After the Council*, trans. David C. Herron and
Rodelinde Albrecht (New York: Herder and Herder, 1966), p. 24.

[2] Edward Schillebeeckx, *The Layman in the Church and Other Essays*, trans.
M. H. Gill (New York: Alba House, 1963), pp. 67–92.

[3] Gregory Baum, *The Credibility of the Church Today* (London: Sheed and
Ward, 1968).

rested on shaky foundations and that, furthermore, it was quite out of accord with the self-understanding of modern man. Davis left the Church for these reasons, but Baum, perhaps surprisingly, has decided to stay in it, chiefly because of Vatican II. He sees in this council a dramatic doctrinal shift which is effectively closing the gap between the faith of Roman Catholicism and the self-consciousness of modern man. Since secularity is no longer the impediment to faith it used to be, the Roman theologian has a whole new mandate and a fresh range of problems to work through.

The new spirit which has become evident in recent years found expression along different lines in feminist-theologian Mary Daly's study entitled *The Church and the Second Sex*.[4] The presence of women in the Roman Church who are vocal about their rights and willing to scold the hierarchy for its anti-feminist ways is not insignificant. Mary Daly's thesis is simple enough, although it is stated somewhat intemperately. There are, she contends, a number of forces in society which have combined to underscore the maltreatment of women: demo-cracy has given women as much significance as men, tech-nology is beginning to minimize the value of brute strength, education is widespread and no longer in the hands of a male *élite*, and industrialization has opened up many new occupa-tional possibilities. Women are emerging as a force to be reckoned with – everywhere except in the Church. The Church, says Mary Daly, is a stronghold of anachronism, a fount of male prejudice and one of the major inspirations for modern antifeminism. In Roman Catholicism, she says, a woman is both idealized and demeaned, but the fact that she is demeaned only points up the hypocrisy in her idealization. The book concludes with some proposals for rectifying this scandalous situation.

It is not entirely clear what direction the new thinking in Catholicism will take. Immediately following the Council, there was a euphoric atmosphere in Roman Catholic circles.

[4] Mary Daly, *The Church and the Second Sex* (London: Chapman, 1968).

The triumph of progressive theology seemed beyond question; the Church no less than its faith would be remade and revitalized. In the last few years, however, the realization of these dreams has become a little less certain.

The history of this period is quite well mirrored in Michael Novak's writing. In 1964, when his book *A New Generation* was published, a certain excitement and optimism ran through its pages.[5] Granted, he said, Roman Catholics at that time were living in one of the ebb-tides of Christian faith. The Church was withdrawn from the world. It was standing aloof, frowning at modern man and, as a result, was unable to communicate its riches to him. However, there had never been a winter which was not followed by a spring. Using another image, he commented that the worm of Roman Catholic faith was about to break out of its cocoon of isolation and take flight in a new faith. The same confident optimism appeared in the other book he brought out entitled *A Time to Build*.[6] Roman Catholic faith was in shambles, but the time had come to repair itself and raise an edifice which would be worthy of God's calling.

In 1971, seven years later, Novak published *All the Catholic People: Where Has All the Spirit Gone?*[7] It was a bittersweet lament about the Church's failure to remake Christian faith in those years. The Spirit has left the Church; the Church is as desolate as before. Novak is deeply disillusioned.

Another index to the new situation created by Vatican II and, perhaps another sign of disillusionment, was the publication of Hans Küng's attack on infallibility.[8] His short-range goal was to attack papal infallibility, but his over-all objective was much larger. He called for a reform 'in head and members' which would root out every claim of infallibility – whether by

[5] Michael Novak, *A New Generation* (New York: Herder and Herder, 1964).
[6] Michael Novak, *A Time to Build* (New York: Macmillan, 1967).
[7] Michael Novak, *All the Catholic People: Where Has All the Spirit Gone?* (New York: Herder and Herder, 1971).
[8] Hans Küng, *Infallible? An Inquiry*, trans. E. Mosbacher (London: Collins, 1971).

the Pope, the Church or the Bible. The concept of infallibility, he feels, is a stubborn obstacle to redefinition of Catholic doctrine. A Protestant attack on infallibility would have passed unnoticed, but since the attack came from one of the leading Catholic theologians, it has attracted wide attention.

Admittedly, few of Küng's colleagues have followed him in his daring criticism. Indeed, many see his actions as a direct assault on the Church. In Küng's favour, it should be said that he believes in the Church's indefectibility if not in its infallibility. He believes, that is, that the Spirit will guide the corporate Church along the path of truth but that the Church will not have the luxury of infallible signposts to strengthen its faith. But even Karl Rahner, who has stood shoulder to shoulder with Küng on other matters, finds this difficult to accept. Küng, Rahner has said, is speaking like a 'Liberal Protestant'. G. C. Berkouwer, the conservative Dutch theologian, is right in seeing that 'the problem Küng puts on the agenda cannot be solved by summoning up the traditional stand. The problem will stay there, and will finally be decisive for the future of Roman Catholicism.'[9] This is so because the myth of an unchanging Catholicism has now been exploded.

[9] G. C. Berkouwer, 'The Küng-Rahner Debate', *Christianity Today*, 15, 7 May 1971, p. 46.

2 ROME'S DIVIDED MIND

The Second Vatican Council is different from the many ecumenical councils which have preceded it[1] in at least two respects. First, it did not result from either external persecution or internal heresy. Second, for the first time in conciliar history, the documents which Vatican II developed officially embraced mutually incompatible theologies. This does not mean that councils in the past have always been unanimous in their decisions, for they have not. Nor does it mean that council decisions were not sometimes compromises, for they were. And it does not mean that individuals or parties in the Church have always interpreted a council's statement in the same way, for they have not.[2] What it means is that this Council actually endorsed two very different theologies and sometimes the differences could not be hidden. Neither side would accept ambiguity or allow compromise. As a result, on some points the documents speak with two voices – one conservative and one progressive. They reflect, in a fascinating and perhaps tragic way, the divided mind of modern Roman Catholicism. As a consequence, they pose a difficult problem. In attempting to analyse the mind of Rome, how are we to interpret the most

[1] For a good account of these councils see Hubert Jedin, *Ecumenical Councils of the Catholic Church: An Historical Outline*, trans. Ernst Graf (Freiburg: Herder, and London: Nelson, 1960).
[2] The classic case of this last kind of difficulty occurred in the fourth century. The council of Nicaea outlawed Arianism, by which the divinity of Christ had been denied, with a statement that He is *homoousios* (of the same substance) with the Father. Having agreed on this word, it took the Church sixty years to decide what was meant. In the meantime different opinions about it developed. The world was then treated to a display of power politics in the Church as the respective parties jostled for position. Bishops clogged the roads galloping from one council to another but all to no avail for more than half a century.

important theological statement to emerge from this Church in this century?

The problem of interpretation will be clarified only when the unresolved confrontation between two opposing theologies is seen clearly. The one theology was traditional, the other was not. The first was championed by the conservatives in general and the Curia in particular, while the second found its proponents among a school of thinkers who in general represent the New Catholicism. The conservative approach largely concerned itself with representing the ideas of the Counter-Reformation and the subsequent periods of high orthodoxy. By contrast, the new thinkers are considerably more flexible in their approach and, compared to traditional orthodoxy, relatively undogmatic. Their theology is rooted more in the patristic period than in the Counter-Reformation, though it was mainly from the developments of the 1940s and early 1950s that they received their new direction. At issue in the Council, then, were not only matters of theology, but also questions of ideology, mentality and almost theological heritage.

When these two parties in the Council came into conflict, as they frequently did, one of three solutions was followed. Occasionally, but rarely, one of the positions emerged completely triumphant. Its ideas were written into the Council documents without modification from the other side.

A second solution was less satisfactory. When neither side would back down and both insisted on having their views adopted, the Council searched for a reconciling statement which would be ambiguous enough to accommodate both schools of thought. When the Council was successful, both viewpoints were represented in one statement which obviously meant different things to different people. An excellent illustration of this second tactic is the Council's treatment of biblical inerrancy to which we will return presently. There were times, however, when no reconciling statement could be found, and attempts to induce a surrender by the one side or the other failed. In those cases, the Council would only endorse both positions with professional aplomb as if their mutual incompatibility was no longer glaringly obvious. A case in point occurred in the constitution on the Church which, as we shall see later, was dramatically highlighted by Pope Paul VI's clumsy intervention.

One kind of interpretative problem, then, which an analyst of the documents faces concerns the existence of those passages which are so brilliantly ambiguous as to be capable of serving the interest of both parties. The statement on biblical inerrancy best illustrates this problem. The Council affirmed:

> Since everything asserted by the inspired authors or sacred writers must be held to be asserted by the Holy Spirit, it follows that the books of Scripture must be acknowledged as teaching firmly, faithfully, and without error that truth which God wanted put into the sacred writings for the sake of our salvation.[3]

This statement, over which there was a considerable tussle both in private and in public, seems at first sight to reaffirm Rome's traditional stance on this matter. For this reason, conservatives in the Council agreed to it, and some Protestants subsequently have been led to think that Catholicism's historic stance on this matter is unaltered.

Rome's former position on biblical inerrancy is at least clear, however wise or unwise it may be. In 1546, for example, the Council of Trent declared its confidence in Scripture 'as having been dictated either orally by Christ or by the Holy Ghost, and preserved in the Catholic Church in unbroken succession'.[4] Inspiration was related to those matters upon which faith depended, which, in the sixteenth century, meant the assertions of Scripture about history no less than its religious teaching. Similarly, in 1864, the Syllabus of Errors declared it was a grievous error to think that 'divine revelation is imperfect, and, therefore subject to continual and indefinite progress which

---

[3] *Con. Revelation*, 11.
[4] *Canons and Decrees of the Council of Trent*, ed. H. J. Schroeder (St Louis: Herder Book Co., 1960), p. 17.

corresponds with the progress of human reason.'[5] Six years
later, the First Vatican Council of 1870 reaffirmed this position,
explaining that the Scriptures must be held as sacred, 'not
because, having been carefully composed by mere human
industry, they were afterwards approved by her authority, nor
merely because they contain revelation, with no admixture of
error, but because, having been written by the inspiration of
the Holy Ghost, they have God for their author. . . .'[6] At the
turn of the century, when some Modernists[7] offered the opinion
that Scripture contained errors, the reigning Pope responded
in a sharply worded encyclical, *Pascendi dominici gregis*,[8] roundly
rebuking them for their views. He then excommunicated the
leaders of the Modernist movement.

The statement which Vatican II produced evidently picked
up the threads of this unambiguous position to which Rome
has always committed herself. Indeed, in a meticulous textual
comparison of the Constitution on Revelation from Vatican I
and that from Vatican II, René Latourelle has shown that
many of the words, phrases and grammatical constructions
from 1870 reappeared in the Vatican II statement.[9] Without
doubt, it would seem, the Roman Catholic Church wants to
say it still believes in biblical inerrancy, at least as it was
defined in 1870. But is this really the case? A careful scrutiny

[5] '*The Encyclical Letter of Pius IX, 8th December, 1964, Proclaiming the Jubilee of
1865; with the Syllabus of LXXX. Errors which He Condemns* (Edinburgh:
George McGibbon, n.d.), p. 5.

[6] *Con. De Rev.*, cap. II.

[7] Hilaire Bourdon [George Tyrrell], *The Church and the Future* (Edinburgh:
Turnbull and Spears, 1903), p. 141.

[8] 'We, Venerable Brethren, for whom there is but one and only truth and
who hold that the Sacred Books, written under the inspiration of the Holy
Ghost, have God for their author . . . say with Augustine: "In an authority
so high, admit but one officious lie, and there will not remain a single
passage of these appparently difficult to practise or to believe, which on the
same most pernicious rule may not be explained as a lie uttered by the
author willfully to serve a purpose" ' (*Encyclical Letter (Pascendi Gregis) of our
Most Holy Lord Pius X by Divine Providence Pope, on the Doctrines of the Modernists*
(London: Burns and Oates, 1907), pp. 44–45).

[9] René Latourelle, *Theology of Revelation* (Oxford: Blackwell, 1968), pp. 453–
480.

of the Council's statement shows that it can be interpreted in an entirely different way, one which a majority of Catholic scholars are now following. In perhaps the most lucid account of the Council's theology, B. C. Butler, the English bishop and progressive theologian, explains how. The Council obviously spoke of the Bible 'teaching without error', but the significance of this phrase, he argues, depends on the view taken of 'the truth' which Scripture is said to teach without error. 'Here the word "truth" is qualified by a statement of the finality or purpose of inspiration; it is a question of truth relevant to God's saving purpose summed up in Christ.'[1] The point he is making is that many truths of science and history have no part to play in our salvation. 'For instance,' he says, 'the date of the appearance of the human species in natural history is not formally relevant to our salvation; the reality of Christ's death and resurrection is formally relevant.'[2]

The illustration in the first half of Butler's sentence is so obvious that the reader is disarmed against the thrust of the second half. The Council's statement, he argues, guarantees as inerrant only those truths necessary for our salvation. The meaning of the passage, therefore, turns on the question of how much we need to know with certainty to be saved. Apparently there is room for discussion on this point. Butler has limited the inerrant statements of Scripture to those which bear on the saving actions of God which were summed up in Christ, but Gregory Baum has trimmed this core even further. To be saved, he says, we need to know exceedingly little; exceedingly little, then, is inerrantly taught in Scripture.

Speaking for the progressive wing in the Catholic Church, Butler says that this interpretation of the Council's statement enjoys two decided advantages over the old view. First, it gives us a different and, he thinks, better conception of truth. Second, it 'rescues exegesis from the impasse created by the

[1] B. C. Butler, *The Theology of Vatican II* (London: Darton, Longman and Todd, 1967), p. 56.
[2] *Ibid.*

apparent contrast between the "inerrancy" which theologians have inferred from the inspiration of Scripture and the findings of modern scientific scholarship.'[3]

Far from placing bounds on adventurous biblical critics in the Roman Church, the Council now appears to offer them positive encouragement. They have not been slow to perceive this. Hans Küng quickly fell into line with the views of Protestant Ernst Käsemann, who is by most standards an extreme critic. Küng and Käsemann are agreed that Scripture contains a mass of conflicting theological traditions.[4] The critics' task is that of weaving some order into these diverse strands and of discarding what is not evidently authentic. Subsequently, in *Infallible? An Inquiry*, Küng has even abandoned the meagre core of infallible truth in Scripture which he formerly respected. The traditional stance which the Church has adopted, he argues, is yet another piece of evidence showing that the Pope is not infallible!

This does not mean that Küng refuses to allow Scripture to determine his theological formulations. As a matter of fact, his books are filled with references to the biblical Word, the reason being, apparently, that he regards records of encounter with Christ as somewhat infallible. This view of Scripture is similar to that of Brunner, the proponent of European neo-orthodoxy. For both theologians, the purpose of the biblical Word is to mediate Christ, and a certain infallibility pertains to this existential encounter with Christ. It is the infallibility of religious encounter rather than that of the biblical text that Küng allows.

Why, then, refer to Scripture at all? Küng does so, not to give his theology a quality of inviolability, but because using biblical ideas is the nearest the theologian can come to describing the reality of God and Christ. The theologians' statement,

---

[3] *Ibid.*, p. 57.
[4] Hans Küng, *The Living Church: Reflections on the Second Vatican Council*, trans. Cecily Hastings and M. D. Smith (London: Sheed and Ward, 1963), pp. 257–259.

however, no less than that of the Bible itself, must ever remain defective. The insufficiency of theological statements is acknowledged by most; the insufficiency, indeed defectiveness, of the biblical statements can only be asserted if the Church's former teaching on this matter is rejected. A less radical, but nevertheless important, summary of the new view is also heralded in the title of one of Karl Rahner's books, *Inspiration in the Bible*.[5]

The frustrating element for the interpreter of the Vatican II documents is that the new approach to inerrancy can apparently be *justified* or *denied* from the same statement. The Council's statement serves as a summary for two views on biblical inerrancy: one restricts the concept to certain aspects of biblical thought and the other does not. Which interpretation is correct? Do we follow the minority in the Council who say that the inerrancy statement must be taken at face value and interpreted in the light of tradition? Or do we follow the majority who show a certain respect for the concept as historically understood but then undermine it through a process of subtle reinterpretation? The inerrancy passage is by no means the only one in the Council documents which poses this problem for the interpreter. It must be said that this situation makes Hans Küng's recent plea for truthfulness in the Church germane and timely.[6]

The existence of passages as ambiguous as these represents an attempt by the Church to maintain a façade of unity. When this became impossible, however, the conflicting theologies were simply laid side by side without any attempt in the document at reconciliation.

In this connection, a most extraordinary event occurred when the Council tried to formulate the doctrine of the Church. The conservative and progressive conceptions simply could not be reconciled, and neither side would retract their ideas. As a result, both sides were successful in having their position

---

[5] Karl Rahner, *Inspiration in the Bible* (New York: Herder and Herder, 1961).
[6] Hans Küng, *Truthfulness: The Future of the Church*, trans. Edward Quinn (London: Sheed and Ward, 1968).

included, although, with the exception of chapter three in the Constitution on the Church, the document largely endorses progressive ideas.[7] The upshot of this endorsement, as we shall see later, is that papal authority has been seriously undermined. Pope Paul deemed the situation sufficiently ominous to warrant his personal intervention. After the Constitution had passed through the Council, he inserted into the document a passage which is called an explanation – '*Nota explicativa Praevia*'. What the note actually explains is not the Council's teaching, but rather the conservative position in general and the contents of Pope Paul's mind in particular. In fact, it contradicts the major part of the Constitution. It repudiates the progressives' doctrine of the Church at its key points. Since Pope Paul's 'explanation' was added to the document after the Council had completed its work, a Council vote on its merits and validity was impossible.

It is plain, once again, that this situation creates serious problems for us as readers. How do we interpret the Constitution on the Church? Do we side with the progressive majority, accepting their position in its wholeness, ignoring that which contradicts it from the conservative side? Or do we take our cue from the legal head of the Church and, on his authority, ignore the major part of the document? There is no easy way out of this impasse.

The existence of these two theologies in the documents explains why some progressive theologians, in private, are now predicting that Vatican III is already on the horizon. It will take place, they say, not much later than 1980. At this time, they feel, the progressive viewpoint will enjoy sufficiently widespread acceptance in the Church that the new Council will be able to rewrite its theology *wholly* in terms of the progressive stance. Vatican III, then, will not be forced into the doctrinal

[7] The clearest analysis of this situation is given in an essay by George A. Lindbeck, 'A Protestant Point of View', *Vatican II: An Interfaith Appraisal*, ed. John H. Miller (Notre Dame: University of Notre Dame Press, 1966), pp. 219–230. The same contention is also sustained in his book *The Future of Catholic Theology* (London: SPCK, 1970).

compromises and ambiguities of Vatican II. Vatican II, as
they see it, is merely the means of transition from 'old-world' to
'new-world' Catholicism. It is simply a stepping stone between
the two orders.[8]

My position in the chapters which follow is that the significance of Vatican II can best be discerned if the progressives'
thinking is kept in mind. Vatican II is important because it
gave the New Catholicism a legal base from which to operate.
If this analysis is correct, the conservative, traditional position,
partly endorsed in the conciliar documents, belongs to a dying
world.[9] The future is not in the hands of the conservatives and
even less under the control of Pope Paul VI.

[8] *Cf.* Küng's statement on the effects of the Council's divided mind: 'We are
now paying – as might have been foreseen – for the inconsistencies arising
from the compromises (unworkable in practice) sought for the sake of the
greatest possible unanimity: compromises between the conciliar majority,
eager for renewal but often anxious and weak, and the curial minority,
efficiently controlling the machinery of the Council' (Küng, *Truthfulness*,
p. 3). This unworkable solution persists, he argues, because traditionalists
have refused to capitulate to progressives. The reverse, of course, is equally
true, but Küng does not pause to consider this. 'Rome – in spite of some
reform-measures and new personalities – is still regarded as a center not of
conciliar renewal but of pre-conciliar resistance' (*ibid.*, p. 5). But he has no
doubt about the eventual outcome of this struggle. He speaks of the 'unshakable hope' which he has 'that the Catholic Church will emerge renewed
even from the post-conciliar crises' (*ibid.*, p. 1).
[9] This theme has precipitated a deluge of literature of both Catholic and
Protestant origin. One example, to which many others could be added, is
W. H. van de Pol, *The End of Conventional Christianity*, trans. Theodore
Zuydwijk (New York: Newman Press, 1967).

3 AUTHORITY:
INWARD OR OUTWARD?

The equilibrium of the Catholic Church has been disturbed during the last four years by the presence of 'Catholic pentecostals'. What is disturbing about them, from an official point of view, is that they show no signs of leaving the Church on the one hand, nor of curbing their novel religious habits on the other. 'Publicly austere but privately ecstatic in their devotion to the Holy Spirit,' says *Time* magazine, 'they remain loyal to the Church but unsettle some of the hierarchy.'[1]

Kevin and Dorothy Ranaghan begin their account of Catholic pentecostalism by quoting an excerpt from the *National Catholic Reporter*: 'To many it seemed incongruous that a movement previously associated with lower class Protestantism and fundamentalism should take root in a Catholic university [Notre Dame] ablaze with the progressive light of the Vatican Council.'[2] There are, it is true, incongruities in the situation. Many serious differences exist between the new pentecostals and the progressives of Vatican II. The quasi-fundamentalism of the one contrasts sharply with the secularizing tendencies of the other. The simple faith of the former is antithetical to the radical doubt of the latter. And even in regard to the Church, the pentecostals are far more loyal to its authority and official teaching than are the liberals.

As great as these differences are, however, there is an area of

[1] 'The New Rebel Cry: Jesus is Coming!' *Time*, 21 June 1971, p. 59.
[2] Kevin and Dorothy Ranaghan, *Catholic Pentecostals* (Parmus, N.J.: Paulist Press, 1969), p. 1. See also Josephine M. Ford, *The Pentecostal Experience* (Parmus: Paulist Press, 1970) and Prudencio Damboriena, *Tongues as of Fire: Pentecostalism in Contemporary Christianity* (Washington: Corpus Books, 1969).

unwitting agreement between the two groups which neither
the Ranaghans nor the *National Catholic Reporter* has noticed.
The point of contact between them is a profound concern with
subjective experience, a concern which is pursued even at the
expense of external authority. The pentecostals are not quite
so eager to negate traditional authority as the progressives,
and the progressives are not quite so interested in pursuing the
inner light as the pentecostals. In fact, since it lacks the
dynamic, experimental quality evident in pentecostal life, the
progressive's experience is probably better described merely as
religious insight. Nonetheless, by entirely different routes and
for entirely different reasons, charismatic and liberal Catholics
have arrived at much the same point. For both, inner realities
are taking precedence over outward authority.

This development is causing deep consternation in traditional
circles. After all, by definition a Roman Catholic lives by the
teaching of his Church. Obedience to Church authority has
always been the central virtue. To disregard this is to begin
dismantling the whole machinery by which millions live – or
so it seems.[3] In addition, Roman Catholics are not free to

---

[3] The backbone of this idea is apostolic succession. Bishops have succeeded
the apostles, not only because they have come after them, but also because
they have inherited apostolic power. And apostolic authority cannot be
ignored or disputed. This aspect of the traditional argument was reaffirmed
by the Council: 'To the Lord was given all power in heaven and on earth.
As successors of the apostles, bishops receive from Him the mission to teach
all nations and to preach the Gospel to every creature. ... To fulfil this
mission, Christ the Lord promised the Holy Spirit to the apostles ...'
(*Con. Revelation*, 24). 'For the discharging of such great duties, the apostles
were enriched by Christ with a special outpouring of the Holy Spirit, who
came upon them (*cf*. Acts 1:8; 2:4; John 20:22–23). This spiritual gift ...
has been transmitted down to us in episcopal consecration' (*ibid.*, 21). On
the historical aspects of this position the best critical essay is still J. B. Lightfoot, 'The Christian Ministry', *Saint Paul's Epistle to the Philippians* (London:
Macmillan, 1888), pp. 181–269. A recent attempt to update Lightfoot's
work by Walter Schmithals, *The Office of the Apostle in the Early Church*, trans.
John E. Steely (London: SPCK, 1971), is largely vitiated by his Bult-
mannian perspective. The importance of the issue, though, is well focused in
Norval Geldenhuys, *Supreme Authority: The Authority of the Lord, His Apostles
and the New Testament* (Grand Rapids: Eerdmans, 1953).

wander down any doctrinal path which might prove inviting, personal insight or subjective experience not withstanding. They belong to an historical Church, one whose future path is predetermined by its past history. Roman Catholic thinking in the present must always be able to justify itself in terms of the doctrine evolved in the past. How, then, can these two movements, so different and yet at one point so alike, justify their departure from traditional life and doctrine?[4]

It is doubtful whether many charismatic Catholics have tried to answer this question. They usually reason non-traditionally and untheologically, and so the mind-set behind the question is alien to their own thinking. As conventional Roman Catholics, they probably reached the point where external authority and teaching seemed increasingly remote and arid. The Church seemed to offer them little hope of satisfying the inner needs of the spirit. No doubt it was all true in theory, but where was its existential validation? How could one know experientially that it was true? The answer to this nagging sense of inner vacuity was not, it seemed, in more earnest obedience to traditional teaching. The validation came, in one or way another, in an encounter with the Spirit. The vital complement to the external authority of the Church was found in the charismatic movement. The former dryness of soul was satisfied in the springs flowing from God in Christ. Without this factor, Roman faith would have died for pentecostal Catholics; with it, official belief has been made to live – at arm's length.

For those progressives with a more theological bent, however, the question is a good deal more complex. Being a Roman Catholic has meant belonging to a rigid historical community. The question was, How could progressives emancipate themselves from the mass of traditional beliefs they felt were smothering them, while at the same time adhering to the essence or core

[4] The best discussion of the technical aspects of this problem is to be found in J. P. Mackey, *The Modern Theology of Tradition* (London: Darton, Longman and Todd, 1965). See also Joseph R. Geiselmann, *The Meaning of Tradition*, trans. W. J. O'Hara (London: Search Press, 1966).

of these beliefs? To find an answer to this seemingly unanswer-
able problem, they went back to John Henry Newman.

Newman was a nineteenth-century Anglo-Catholic who
seceded to Rome[5] and then propounded many of the seminal
ideas which came to maturity at Vatican II. This was not the
first time Newman was appealed to by theological innovators.
Catholic Modernists tried to use him at the turn of the century,
and a large-scale revival of interest in Newman is similarly
under way today. Newman himself would probably be appre-
hensive about these developments. He was wary of those of
liberal persuasion, whether they were theologians or politicians.
But it does seem as if he unwittingly provided the means
whereby progressive Catholics are now liberating themselves
from the heavy load of traditional belief.

The Second Vatican Council validated at least two of
Newman's central theses. Newman had argued that Scripture
has reduced only a part of special revelation to written form;
there is also non-propositional revelation which has not been
'inscripturated'. Through the mind, the Christian has access
to the written revelation and through intuition to the unwritten
revelation. There are not, however, two sources of revelation.
That which is perceived intuitively fills in the gaps and puts
flesh on the ribs of that which has been committed to writing.
They belong together.

The Council, first of all then, accepted Newman's idea of
intuition. Every Christian, it taught, possesses this faculty
which gives him access to revelation not explicit in the biblical
Word. Newman had called this 'real assent'; Vatican II calls
it the 'perception of faith' (sensus fidei).[6] It is a perception
similar to what the sixteenth-century Anabaptists, who were on

[5] Newman's own account of this is given in an autobiography entitled
Apologia Pro Vita Sua (London: Dent, Everyman Library, 1967). Useful
collateral and background material on Newman is to be found in Günter
Biemer, *Newman on Tradition*, trans. K. Smyth (London: Sheed and Ward,
1967) and Charles Stephen Dessain, *John Henry Newman* (London: Nelson,
1966).
[6] *Con. Church*, 12, 35; *Past. Con. Church World*, 52.

the radical fringe of the Reformation, had called the 'inner Word' (*internum verbum*).[7] It is what Fox and the Quakers were to describe as the 'inner light'. It is an inner conviction (regarding some divine truth) which comes to a Christian, through prayer, ecstasy or meditation. The existence of this faculty, which in the past was not accentuated and was always subject to authority, provides the means of liberation from traditional formulations.

Second, the Council also validated Newman's idea that revelation is progressing. The Council said that the progress is not so much in the revelation itself as in the Church's understanding of it, but it seems to have been stated in this way merely out of deference to the traditional past. What is actually meant is that revelation which was formerly hidden in the Scripture is being increasingly revealed and must therefore increasingly affect the total content of written revelation. The passage in which all this is explained states:

> This tradition which comes from the apostles develops in the Church with the help of the Holy Spirit. For there is a growth in the understanding of the realities and the words which have been handed down. This happens through the contemplation and study made by believers who treasure these things in their hearts (*cf*. Luke 2:19, 51), through the intimate understanding of spiritual things they experience, and through the preaching of those who have received through the episcopal succession the sure gift of truth. For, as the centuries succeed one another, the Church constantly moves forward toward the fullness of divine truth until the words of God reach their complete fulfillment in her.[8]

Two important but apparently contradictory ideas are taught in these words. On the one hand, the passage seems to endorse the Protestants' 'Scripture alone' (*sola scriptura*) position. The Church's doctrine is built only around 'the

[7] Recent study has shown that many diverse groups are covered by the elastic term of 'Anabaptist'. The classic study on the movement is that of George H. Williams, *The Radical Reformation* (Philadelphia: Westminster Press, 1962). The Anabaptists mentioned here represent a section of the movement which was singled out for attack by the Reformers.

[8] *Con. Revelation*, 8.

words of God'. On the other hand, it seems to intimate that
revelation (the part not committed to writing) is progressing.
The Church, it is said, 'moves toward the fullness of divine
truth', which can only mean that divine truth in its fullness
is not now in her possession. This certainly is not like the *sola
scriptura* position. The Reformers never claimed to have an
exhaustive knowledge of biblical truth, but they did maintain
that any 'new truth' arises out of the Spirit's application of the
Word in the Christian's life. The 'new truth' in no way adds
to that in Scripture.

It is interesting to note that the Constitution on Revelation
begins with a quotation, not of 2 Timothy 3:16, as one might
have expected, but from 1 John 1:2–3: 'We announce to you
the eternal life. . . .' In the next article, revelation is identified
with the experience of grace.[9] A little later, lest readers should
be in any doubt about the point, revelation is subsumed under
the experience of receiving the gospel.[1] Divine life and (non-
biblical) divine revelation, the Council was saying, are implicated in one another and experienced together. Writing of this,
Tavard has explained that:

> Revelation is neither essentially a doctrine, although it implies one;
> nor a set of propositions and formulations to be believed, although
> it may be partially expressed in such propositions; nor the promul-
> gation of an ethical law of prescriptions, although it also implies
> judgement of the morality of human behaviour. Essentially revela-
> tion is a life. It is the very life of God imparted to man through the
> incarnation of the Son; it is the communication of God's Word
> understood by man in the Holy Spirit.[2]

What is spoken of as 'revelation' is really insight which arises
out of religious experience. The Constitution does endorse a
traditional view of Scripture, but progressives have focused

---

[9] *Ibid.*, 2.
[1] *Ibid.*, 7.
[2] George H. Tavard, *The Dogmatic Constitution on Divine Revelation of Vatican
Council II, Promulgated by Pope Paul VI, November 18, 1965 – Commentary and
Translation* (London: Darton, Longman and Todd, 1966), p. 17.

much of their attention on the unwritten and intuitive aspect which they also call revelation.

So that we can see better the direction in which the progressives are moving, it is worth taking our bearings from the historic Protestant view on Scripture. Unfortunately, there is still much misunderstanding about the Reformation view despite the clarity with which the Reformers spoke on this matter. Some scholars, such as John McNeil and Rupert Davies,[3] have contended that there was some hesitation on the part of the Reformers either to endorse a trustworthy Bible or to affirm that special revelation has become coincidental with the written text of Scripture. However, the arguments and evidence advanced and arrayed against this contention by Michael Reu,[4] Skevington Wood[5] and Kenneth Kantzer[6] seem far more convincing. According to the Reformers, special revelation is complete in Scripture; according to the new Catholic position, it is still in process of unfolding. The Reformers asserted that our religious experience always stands in judgment under Scripture; the progressives maintain it is the means by which the bare ribs of Scripture are receiving some flesh. The first position views inspiration as something which far surpassed, though it in no way suspended, the writer's natural abilities.[7] The second position easily lends itself to the idea that Scripture is little more than the writer's account of his mystical experience. But, because the writer's fallibility intrudes between them, the experience and the written account never quite coincide. Scripture, then, is a record of a remarkable series of events, but it is only a secondary account and, as

[3] Rupert Davies, *The Problem of Authority in the Continental Reformers* (London: Epworth, 1946).
[4] Michael Reu, 'Luther and the Scriptures', *The Springfielder*, 24, Aug. 1960, 9–112.
[5] A. Skevington Wood, *Captive to the Word: Martin Luther, Doctor of Sacred Scripture* (Exeter: Paternoster, 1969).
[6] Kenneth Kantzer, 'Calvin and the Holy Scriptures', *Inspiration and Interpretation*, ed. John Walvoord (Grand Rapids: Eerdmans, 1957).
[7] See Clark H. Pinnock, *Biblical Revelation: The Foundation of Christian Theology* (Chicago: Moody, 1971), pp. 53–106.

such, fallible. The biblical critic has the task of uncovering the 'truth', the original experience, and this, as it often turns out, is very different from the record given of it in the biblical Word.

This raises an important question. In view of the concern with subjective realities among both pentecostal and progressive Catholics, what significance does the teaching of Scripture have, when taken in a historico-grammatical sense?

To answer this question, we turn to the Ranaghans' book first. There is no doubt that it reveals what earlier popes would have called 'doctrinal indifferentism'. The ideas which they extol are often justified on the basis of experience rather than biblical doctrine. It is true that references are made to Scripture in the middle chapters of the book, but what is said there is somewhat nullified by the Ranaghans' over-all attitude to biblical doctrine. In an appendix, for example, it is seriously argued that 'the values of pentecostalism as a meaningful and valid part of Christianity can be approached from both the theological left and right'.[8] By the 'left' they apparently have in mind radicals similar to John Robinson and Rudolf Bultmann who have discarded the plain teaching of Scripture – on matters such as life after death, the resurrection, atonement, salvation and Christ's return. By the 'right' they have in mind those who accept Scripture at its face value, in its plain and evident sense. Nevertheless, they claim, regardless of what a person believes, he can enter into the pentecostal experience.

The more one reflects on this idea, the more unacceptable it appears. After all, there is a whole set of presuppositions lying behind Christian experience in a biblical framework. A relationship with Christ today presupposes the belief that Christ has risen and is present in His Church; that His death was sufficient to open the presence of God to sinners from whom this had been barred; that the Spirit, the third person of the triune God, has been shed upon the Church; that through the Spirit an inner union has been effected between Christ, the Bridegroom, and the body of Christians, His bride; and that this

[8] Ranaghan, p. 261.

union is registered on the total being – heart, mind and will. Assume all of this, and religious experience becomes a possibility. But, according to the Ranaghans, you need assume little or none of it and religious experience, indeed charismatic experience, will still be possible. What is important is the experience itself, regardless of the framework within which it is placed because religious experience provides its own framework. The teaching of Scripture is useful in so far as it coincides with the illumination which experience brings, but it is not always central in determining how experience should take place. The Bible is used in much the same way as a drunk uses a lamppost.

An almost identical feeling about religious experience is to be found among progressives, although on the surface they are most insistent about the need to return to Scripture. What they seem to have in mind, however, is a return to that experience of which Scripture is a record. Some who are in the van of the progressive movement, like Hans Küng, are also leaders in Catholic biblical criticism. Küng, for example, often repeats his call for a return to the Word, but Scripture, he has said, contains a mass of contradictory doctrines, some of which are false.[9]

So, charismatic and liberal Catholics find themselves in agreement on one matter at least. But the fact that these two movements should then diverge in different directions is a clear indication that subjective experience or religious insight, by itself, is notoriously unreliable as a guide to truth. Evidently

[9] The appeal for renewal has taken the form of a return to the original sources of Roman Catholicism, meaning Scripture and the theology of the early Fathers. Thus a new beginning is again possible and the historic route which Catholic thought took through Thomas Aquinas and the medieval Schoolmen can be largely ignored. This explains the head-on collision which took place in the Council over the place of Thomas Aquinas' thought in seminary training. Progressives refused to admit the phrase 'Sancto Thoma Magistro' into the text on the ground that they revered Thomas but would not mutely follow his leadership. They took this line despite the overwhelming weight of over one hundred encyclicals enforcing Thomistic thought on the Church. 'There is no surer sign that a man is tending to Modernism,' one encyclical had said, 'than when he begins to show his dislike for the scholastic method' (Pascendi, 53).

missing are firm controls over religious experience. This will also become clear in some of the chapters which follow.

In spite of the novelty of the current religious situation, it is instructive to note that the options probed in the sixteenth century are still alive today. Maintaining one position was the Roman Catholicism against which Luther and Calvin revolted. The Church at that time argued for two sources of revelation, Scripture and tradition.[1] A second option was provided by some of the Anabaptists who, even if they were not quite as explicit in their beliefs, nevertheless acted on the basis of two sources of revelation, Scripture and subjective insight. The Reformers provided a third option, objecting to both the Roman and the Anabaptist positions. In neither case, they said, was Scripture free to proclaim its message unhindered. In the one case, it was free to speak only so far as tradition allowed; in the other, it was free to speak only so far as esoteric insight had validated it. But in neither case did it have its own intrinsic authority to judge both tradition and experience where they departed from its teaching.

The terms of this debate have not changed – only the balance of the parties. The traditional Roman Catholic stance on Scripture and tradition has been abandoned by virtually everyone. But, instead of moving to the Reformers' position, it would appear that many Catholics have become rather more Anabaptistic.

This shift does not mean either that Anabaptists and their Catholic friends are alone concerned with the experience of the Spirit or that historic Protestantism is not. At issue is the place which this experience should have and the authority which

[1] In an attempt to forget the traditional past, some theologians have stoutly denied this. The denial is made on flimsy evidence at best and certainly in the centuries which followed, official Roman Catholic thought understood the Council of Trent to have taught this. This is why the first draft of the Constitution on Revelation at Vatican II offered a schema in which there were two sources of revelation proposed. See the discussion on this and related points in G. C. Berkouwer, *The Second Vatican Council and the New Catholicism*, trans. L. B. Smedes (Grand Rapids: Eerdmans, 1965), pp. 89–111.

should be given to Scripture in controlling Christian life and thought.

In the Bible's self-witness, the revelation of the Word and the work of the Spirit should complement each other. The Spirit's work is not to bring fresh revelation or new truth. We have God's finished revelation in Scripture. Rather, the Spirit authenticates this teaching, personalizing it, applying it to us directly, and throwing light into the inner recesses of our being. Scripture provides the objective factor in religious experience, and this preserves us from false teaching. The Spirit provides us with the subjective factor, and this preserves us from coldness and apathy. If we ignore Scripture, making experience our criterion of truth, we will be at the mercy of doctrinal pressures which could lead us far from the Christ in whom we wish to believe; if we ignore the Spirit, if we have credence without commitment, we will become guilty of that empty pretence which Scripture calls hypocrisy.[2]

In the sixteenth century, the recovery of this twofold truth – the Spirit and the Word – led to the recovery of the lost knowledge of God. The gospel of grace, hidden in the pages of Scripture and illuminated by the Holy Spirit, was found. This can and should be our experience too.

[2] Faith (*pistis*) in the New Testament evidently balances the need for both objective and subjective factors. The mind is involved, no less than the emotions and will. Faith consists partly of intellectual conviction (Phil. 1:27; 2 Cor. 4:13; 1 Tim. 1:19; 6:20; 2 Thes. 2:13; Jude 3, 20), but never of intellectual credence alone. Accompanying this knowledge and induced by it is an inward trust in Christ (Jn. 1:12; 3:14–15, 18–21; 5:40; 7:37; 6:44; Rom. 2:7; 3:22–25; 4:5; 5:1–2; Gal. 2:16; Eph. 2:8; 3:12). Arising out of the conjunction of belief and commitment is that assurance of which the writer to the Hebrews spoke when he said that 'faith is the assurance of things hoped for, the conviction of things not seen' (Heb. 11:1). See also 1 Cor. 1:21–31; Jn. 16:8–11; Rom. 8:14–17; 1 Jn. 5:9–11. The Reformers summarized this teaching by saying that faith consists of *notitia* (knowledge) on the one side, and *assensus* (the response of the emotions) and *fiducia* (the action of the will) on the other side.

4 GOD: IN THE EARTHLY OR
THE HEAVENLY CITY?

Traditionally, the sacred and the secular have been quite sharply distinguished from one another. Christians have always argued that the life of the earthly city has contributed little to the building of God's kingdom, at least in the sense of bringing men to salvation. This does not mean that the sacred and the secular are wholly unrelated to one another. Reformed, Lutheran and Roman Catholic theology have all sought to show their relationship, though in different ways. In Reformed theology, for example, the relationship of the sacred and the secular has been achieved by means of the notion of 'common grace'. This view maintains that all men are recipients of a measure of grace. It is this fact alone which enables men, who are by nature corrupt, to be benevolent, selfless at times, capable of great artistic achievement, and to be in possession of talents whose use can serve the interests of other men. Although Lutheran theology has accepted the thrust of the Reformed position, it has developed its own notion around the idea of 'calling'. Secular structures, such as they are, are instituted and preserved by God and He calls His children to serve Him in their midst.

It should be noticed, however, that although in both the Reformed and Lutheran schemes secular reality has a significant role to play in Christian life, in neither instance does it by itself lead to salvation. Conversely, a Christian who is 'in' the world is not to derive his values from it (Jn. 17:15–16). Until recently, the respective distinctiveness of the sacred and secular at this point has not been seriously challenged.

Today, however, in both Protestant and Catholic thinking,

an attempt is being made to change this view. A new relationship between the sacred and the secular, between the supernatural and the natural, between God and the world, is being
forged. At the bottom of the new thinking is the knowledge
that the reality of God has been lost in the Church.[1] What is at
issue, therefore, is not whether God has structured secular
reality, for He has, nor whether He enables men to transcend
their sinfulness and utilize their natural gifts, for He does. The
issue is, rather, whether secular reality can bring the saving
presence of God to modern man, whether it should be allowed
to yield a value system for him, and whether he should interpret
himself by its terms.

This concern with secularity has come about because of
the apparent absence of God from the Church. Christians
have waited for Godot and he has never come. Why? The root
cause of the problem, it is felt, is bad philosophy. Traditional
Roman Catholic belief, the new theologians maintain, has
given to the world a concept of God which was derived
primarily from Greek philosophy of the twelfth and thirteenth
centuries.

Traditionally, they say, Catholics have thought of the supernatural and the natural like two layers of a cake. All the two
layers have in common is the single line of demarcation which
separates them. They remain divided. The supernatural cannot
possibly mingle with the natural, for the supernatural is 'above'
the natural. Apart from miraculous intervention, the respective
purity of each sphere is never violated. When miracles occur,
God enters this world almost in the guise of a foreign raider.
After a series of stabs at existing structures, He then disappears.
Since miracles happen so infrequently (if at all), the traditional
Catholic, it is said, is hard put to explain why he believes in
God. After all, for the overwhelming proportion of man's days,
God is in residence elsewhere. Since His residence is far above

[1] Recent statistical evidence on this point with regard to America is supplied
in Rodney Stark and Charles Y. Glock, *American Piety: The Nature of Religious
Commitment* (Berkeley: U. of California, 1968), p. 222.

man's earthly city, God is almost beyond the range of human comprehension and experience.

This false theorizing, the new theologians claim, has evacuated human life of divine reality. The concept of a God 'above' everything is meaningless in an existential and secular age. By failing to see the supernatural *in* the natural, the sacred *in* the secular, God in the world, modern man has accidentally overlooked the presence of God. Change the traditional conception and man will find God again.

These are the themes which run through a number of post-Vatican II publications. In 1966, for example, Leslie Dewart published a book entitled *The Future of Belief*.[2] It proved to be so influential and provocative that in the following year Gregory Baum brought out a sequel[3] containing some of the responses elicited by Dewart's book.

Dewart exposed a raw nerve in the anatomy of contemporary belief. The problem, he asserted, is that modern man finds he can no longer believe in God – as traditionally defined, that is. The reason for this does not lie in the Church's rhetoric; it is not a problem of communications. Nor, for that matter, is it a pastoral problem. Instead, it is a *theoretical* problem. The substance of secular experience simply cannot be squared with the essence of Christian theistic belief, and it is this, he claimed, which is primarily responsible for the widespread restlessness in the Roman Catholic Church.

Dewart dismissed some of the more obvious solutions to the difficulty. To ask secular man to adopt the cultural and religious values of traditional Catholicism would be ridiculous. This is what Karl Marx rightly rejected as 'mystification', said Dewart. Some Roman Catholics have recognized that it is not feasible to ask for a conversion of secular people, so they have tried to live with a foot in both worlds. They live two lives, one

[2] Leslie Dewart, *The Future of Belief: Theism in a World Come of Age* (London: Sheed and Ward, 1967).
[3] Gregory Baum, *The Future of Belief Debate* (New York: Herder and Herder, 1967).

secular and one religious. Living in two separate worlds, they have two modes of existence as distinct and separate from one another as east is from west. This compromise situation, Dewart said, is obviously unsatisfactory.

Some Roman Catholics who would agree with Dewart's judgment have found a different resolution. Accepting the incompatibility of the secular and religious outlooks, they have opted for the latter and completely rejected the former. Often this leads them into the monastic way of life. While this may personally satisfy them, Dewart said, it is no answer to the problem of how the Christian God can be related to the secular world. Dewart claimed that a majority of Roman Catholics today have seen this and have chosen the opposite solution, that of living in the secular city. They have adopted the cultural and ethical values of our secular age. They have become secular men who apparently retain some kind of religious awareness in the back of their minds.

Using this final category as his starting point, Dewart then attempted to analyse how and in what way these people can speak of God and how He can be in relationship with them. The analysis on a somewhat broader front spilled over into Dewart's next book, *The Foundation of Belief*, which was published in 1969.[4] It is sufficient to note, however, that for Dewart the cause of this modern problem of disbelief is really theoretical and intellectual. A 'dehellenization' of the doctrine of God must take place.

Daniel Callahan has argued, quite correctly it would seem, that it was the Council itself which provided the main impulse for this kind of thought in recent years. When the Council decided to deal with the theme of the Church in the modern world, it was almost as if it had awakened from its medieval slumbers to find itself surrounded by secular reality. The Council's constitution, *Gaudium et Spes*, was a green light to Roman Catholic theologians to start coming to terms with secular reality. For Callahan this meant something very similar to what it meant

[4] Leslie Dewart, *The Foundations of Belief* (London: Search Press, 1969).

for Dewart. At any rate, it is significant that Callahan was the
one to gather up the responses to Protestant secularist Harvey
Cox's book *The Secular City*[5] and publish them in a sequel.[6]

In place of this old scheme, a redefinition of the natural
and supernatural is being offered by some of the progressives.
Instead of seeing these two worlds as adjoining but separate
realities, they are suggesting that it is possible to see them as
blended and intermingled in one another. This view, as a
matter of fact, had also come to the surface in the Council's
discussion, although at an unexpected place. In its delibera-
tions over matters of eschatology – life after death, the second
coming of Christ and the end of the world – the Council was
forced to confront this new thinking. The issue presented itself
in a rather odd form: should the axis of eschatology lie vertically or horizontally?

At the cost of oversimplification, the question can be put
another way: is God's salvation effected ultimately through our
resurrection *out* of the world or through our involvement in
secular institutions *in* the world? The former option is the one
adopted by traditionalists and is consistent, it is said, with their
two-layer world. The lower layer is secular and thus provides
the Christian with nothing but an alien and hostile environment. Traditionalists, progressives argue, long to escape it
since the only things meaningful to them belong in the upper
world. As they wait to take flight from the world, they begin
to resemble the nervous hermit weaving and unweaving his
baskets.[7] On this reckoning, the plan of salvation is accomplished vertically through the Christian's extraction *from* the
world. This, of course, puts the options too starkly, but it
indicates how the debate is shaping up.

[5] Harvey Cox, *The Secular City: Secularization and Urbanization in Theological
Perspective* (Harmondsworth: Penguin, 1968).
[6] Daniel J. Callahan, ed., *The Secular City Debate* (London: Collier-
Macmillan, 1966).
[7] Barnabas Ahern, 'The Eschatological Dimensions of the Church', *Vatican
II: An Interfaith Appraisal*, ed. John H. Miller (Notre Dame: U. of Notre
Dame Press), pp. 296–300.

Alternatively, some progressives have argued that God's saving plan is partly identified with secular life and is being realized through it.[8] Redemption is ultimately achieved *in* the world, not *above* it, for the two layers of the cake have become one. No longer is the Christian a lonely hermit in refuge from secular life. On the contrary, human activity at all levels in our society is providing the raw substance for God's redemptive work. Secular man, then, is becoming a co-worker with God in redeeming human life, and the catalyst in this action is the Christian. Thus Barnabas Ahern has explained:

> What really matters is the tremendous truth affirmed by the Council that all worthwhile human activity is part of the creative plan of God and of the redemptive mystery of Christ who died that he might re-establish all things and transform them into the perfect eschatological kingdom of his Father. The whole world – the heavens and the earth, the vast oceans and verdant fields, the tangled bush of Africa and the trampled streets of New York, men of all colors and of all backgrounds – all that God has made is alive with an *élan to God*.[9]

According to this view, eschatology will be realized horizontally rather than vertically. The object of God's saving purposes is not merely the souls of Christian people, but rather human life in all of its parts. Moreover, in order to achieve this end, God is not extracting people *out* of the world, but is presently active *in* the world in all of its comprehensive reality. This means, among other things, that heaven is not going to be somewhere 'out there'. Rather, the present physical earth will be transformed into heaven because it is now being prepared for God's eternal habitation. The home of man is going to become the home of God; the institutions of man likewise will become God's institutions.

[8] Over the last three decades, most of the pioneering in Catholic theology has been done by the French. On this point, see Jean-Marie Domenach and Robert de Montvalon, eds., *The Catholic Avant-Garde: French Catholicism Since World War II* (New York: Holt, Rinehart and Winston, 1967), pp. 6–26, 210–241.
[9] Ahern, p. 299.

Edward Schillebeeckx is among those who have suggested this new approach. In *God the Future of Man*, he has argued that there is a deep chasm dividing modern man's secularity and the the religious ideals of traditional Catholicism.[1] He traces the growth of secularity from the twelfth century onwards and concludes that Christian thought has not kept pace with secular development. Rejecting the notion of two-layered reality, Schillebeeckx goes on to argue that the meaning of God is internal, and its fullest realization will happen on the horizontal sphere of man's own history. Schillebeeckx identifies God with an inner sense which he says men have that the future has meaning. Man has an unshakable confidence that at the end of the road there will be good, not bad. This is God.

Some of these ideas were also probed in a volume edited by Schillebeeckx and entitled *The Problem of Eschatology*.[2] It contains essays by several authors who examine the themes of death, resurrection, immortality and the soul, on the assumption that the afterlife is to occur on the flat plane of man's history and not in some airy world 'above'.

By removing the frontier that has traditionally divided the natural from the supernatural, contemporary theologians are able to see reality as one composite whole.[3] The whole of the created world is beginning to throb with the hidden life of God. It is this development, more than anything else, which explains the current convergence between Eastern and Western thought. This view has profound implications for the doctrine of man, as we shall see, and it is these implications which are leading

[1] Edward Schillebeeckx, *God the Future of Man*, trans. N. D. Smith (New York: Sheed and Ward, 1968).
[2] Edward Schillebeeckx, ed., *The Problem of Eschatology* (New York: Paulist Press, 1969).
[3] The prophet of this development was Teilhard de Chardin, but the most brilliant exponent is Karl Rahner. See, for example, his *Theological Investigations*, trans. Cornelius Ernst, I (London: Darton, Longman and Todd, 1961), pp. 297–347. On Rahner himself, see Louis Roberts, *The Achievement of Karl Rahner* (New York: Herder and Herder, 1967) and Herbert Vorgrimler, *Karl Rahner: His Life, Thought and Works*, trans. Edward Quinn (London: Burns and Oates, 1965).

Western theologians towards Eastern pantheism, mysticism and universalism. The infusion of the supernatural in the natural also explains why some of the distinctives of the Christian doctrine of God, such as His personality, seem less tenable today than before. When the being of God is identified with secularity and even with trees, rivers, grass, streets, buildings and atomic bombs, the idea of His personality becomes difficult to maintain. When this occurs, the personality of man also becomes doubtful. He may be nothing more than a chance collation of atoms, in which case the search for meaning in human life will probably end in failure.

Before looking at these implications more closely, however, we must examine the extent to which the Council endorsed the new eschatology. The universalism implicit in the new view emerges in several important passages in the Council documents, one of which states:

> The Church, to which we are all called in Christ Jesus, and in which we acquire sanctity through the grace of God, will attain her full perfection only in the glory of heaven. Then will come the time of the restoration of all things (Acts 3:21). *Then the human race as well as the entire world ... will be perfectly re-established in Christ* [my italics].[4]

Second, the idea that secular activity is being incorporated into the divine plan of salvation since the dividing wall between God and the world has been partially broken down is taught in the following passage:

> For after we have obeyed the Lord, and in His Spirit nurtured on earth the values of human dignity, brotherhood and freedom, and indeed all the good fruits of our nature and enterprise, *we will find them again* [my italics]. ... This will be so when Christ hands over to the Father a kingdom eternal and universal.[5]

[4] *Con. Church*, 48. Cf. *Past. Con. Church World*, 22, 32, 42, 55; *Decln. Non-Christian*, 1.

[5] *Past. Con. Church World*, 39. 'Faith in Man', Bernard Lambert has commented, 'has been incorporated into faith in God. If man, his history and his life are hidden in Christ, as St Paul says, then cultural life and civilization itself are not estranged from the mystery of Christ. ... Christ is at the heart of our worldly revolution as well as being at the center of development in

Christ's atonement, then, was aimed at restoring earthly institutions no less than broken human natures. Human activity which makes life more genuinely human is bringing us nearer the final consummation because it is making life more genuinely divine. Every technical advance, every adventure into space, every effort to rout crime and every attempt to give capitalism a conscience, if man is really being served, have become means of God's salvation of man. The reality of God has become identified with the reality of the earthly city, the sacred is found *in* the secular, Christ is *in* the world.[6]

This may give the impression that the Council endorsed the new secular theology without reserve. This, of course, is not true. Alongside ideas from the 'horizontal' eschatology were juxtaposed ideas from the more traditional 'vertical' eschatology.[7] The interpreter of the Council's theology is once again in a difficult position. Should conciliar teaching be identified with the first option on the grounds that a majority endorsed it? Or should it be aligned with the second option on the grounds that this teaching seems to have papal approval? The interpretation adopted here is that the new secular theology will either determine the direction in which Catholic thinking will move, despite papal disapproval, or at least it will be highly influential within Catholicism. The reasons for taking this approach are those which were given earlier in trying to decide which theology of revelation should be accepted from the Council's teaching.

---

the whole creation' (Bernard Lambert, 'La Problematique Générale de la Constitution Pastorale', *L'Église dans le monde de ce temps: Constitution Pastorale 'Gaudium et Spes'*, ed. Y. M. J. Congar and M. Peuchmaurd (Paris: Cerf, 1967), II, 167).

[6] On the Protestant side, Harvey Cox has developed this line of thought in his *The Secular City* (Harmondsworth: Penguin, 1968). His thesis has been brilliantly demolished by Jacques Ellul, *The Meaning of the City*, trans. Dennis Pardee (Grand Rapids: Eerdmans, 1970).

[7] In the Constitution on the Church, for example, article 48 discusses the communion that exists between those in heaven above and those on earth below. The former strengthen the latter, so prayers to the dead are encouraged (art. 50). Even the traditional notion of saints is endorsed (art. 51).

In the new thinking, man is the focal point of theological attention. He is, after all, the point of integration between the orders of reality. Through man a bridge is thrown over from the one sphere of reality to the other. Consequently, 'signals of transcendence' register on his inner life. In so far as this is true, religious experience does provide basic theological information for these 'insights', and 'perceptions' can be accepted as a form of revelation. The Council in its Pastoral Constitution on the Church in the Modern World utilized these insights and accepted man's centrality: 'Hence the pivotal point of our total presentation will be man himself, whole and entire, body and soul, heart and conscience, mind and will.'[8]

There are two ways to explain how the nature of man is pervaded by the supernatural. Philosophically, an argument has been developed along the lines of being. Man's being, it is said, runs down into and becomes continuous with Being. Since Being pervades the world, man is an important point of juncture between material and spiritual reality. Alternatively, a more theological approach is possible. Man participates in and is an expression of the divine, not primarily through his being but through his humanity. His humanity is the point of connection with divinity. This seems to be the explanation adopted by the Council, in one passage at least. Speaking of the death of Christ, it was stated:

> To the sons of Adam He restores the divine likeness which had been disfigured from the first sin onward. Since human nature as He assumed it was not annulled by that very fact it has been raised up to a divine dignity in our respect too. *For by His incarnation the Son of God has united Himself in some fashion with every man* [my italics].[9]

For students living in the twentieth century and nurtured largely, if unconsciously, on European existentialism, this statement is at least enigmatic and probably nonsensical. It implies a view of human nature which is alien to our Western

[8] *Past. Con. Church World*, 3.
[9] *Ibid.*, 22.

mentality. For centuries, however, it has been upheld in the Eastern Orthodox Church.

In Greek philosophy, human nature was looked upon as a single and universal phenomenon, a kind of web spread over the whole earth, each man constituting a small part. It was like a universal substance, a minuscule amount of which had been dropped into the crucible of each body. Every person, then, is a partial or pale representation of this total reality, and each person is related to the whole of mankind in a far more binding way than mere blood relationship. For the existentialist, however, this kind of thinking spells the end of individual action and responsibility. For him, each man is an independent island. There is no universal stuff called human nature antecedent to the individual's existence. Consequently the individual comes into the world with an unformed nature. What shape it will eventually take depends on the actions of will by which the man fashions and authenticates himself. There is no relationship between individual men and mankind. Plato summarized the Greek view by saying that essence precedes existence; Sartre rejected it, saying that existence precedes essence.

At this point, the Council showed itself in agreement with Plato rather than Sartre. Did the second person of the Godhead join Himself to Jesus as an isolated individual or to the universal phenomenon of human nature and hence to mankind *in toto*? The Platonic view demands the latter. The Council agreed in at least one place, saying that Christ 'united Himself in some fashion with every man'.

If Christ joined Himself to humanity in the incarnation, rather than to the isolated human nature in Jesus,[1] two

---

[1] Bonhoeffer believed this, too, explaining that 'as they contemplated the miracle of the Incarnation, the early Fathers passionately contended that while it was true to say that God took human nature upon him, it was wrong to say that he chose a perfect individual man and united himself to him. God was made man, and while that means that he took upon him our entire human nature with all its infirmity, sinfulness and corruption, the whole of apostate humanity, it does not mean that he took upon him the man Jesus.

important consequences follow. First, the focus of theology has plainly shifted from Calvary to Bethlehem, from the atonement to the incarnation. The incarnation virtually effects atonement. Union with Christ is effected not through trusting in His saving death but through being organically joined to mankind in whom Christ's life has been released. In much the same way as a pond will slowly become coloured if a bucket of dye is thrown into it, so humanity is slowly being divinized through the life of Christ which has been injected into it at the incarnation.[2]

The second important consequence is that the focus of salvation has shifted from the idea of justification to that of deification. Traditionally in Roman Catholicism, sin has been defined in legal terms. The Reformers also built on this idea. Sin, they argued, is law-breaking. Under the law's condemnation, man becomes powerless to release himself. Justification, the act of release, was similarly couched in legal terms. God the judge, they taught, releases man from his legal offence and imputes his crime to and exacts his punishment on another. It is true, of course, that this represents only one aspect of the Bible's teaching: the event of being saved involves much more than these bare legal exchanges. Nevertheless, it does not involve less than these.

However, some passages of the conciliar documents define sin more as a clouding of our minds through our mortality than as a perverting of our natures through moral disobedience. Sin, it is said, is internal 'imbalance';[3] salvation, we conclude, consists in introducing the principle of immortality into human

Unless we draw this distinction we shall misunderstand the whole message of the gospel. *The Body of Jesus Christ, in which we are taken up with the whole human race, has now become the ground of our salvation'* [my italics] (Dietrich Bonhoeffer, *The Cost of Discipleship*, trans. R. H. Fuller (London: SCM Press, 1959), p. 213).

[2] On the Protestant side, Thomas Altizer was the forerunner of this theme in his *Gospel of Christian Atheism* (London: Collins, 1967).

[3] In the Council's documents sin is more often dealt with in terms of its consequences than in terms of its nature. Nevertheless, if the manifestations of sin are called 'imbalances' (*Past. Con. Church World*, 8), so the sundering

life which will then reverse the effects of imbalance in mortality. The life of Christ which is the immortal yeast in the mortal human dough will eventually permeate every man. As this occurs, a man becomes more genuinely human and as he becomes more genuinely human, he becomes more genuinely divine. The new eschatology seems to assume as its salvation-model the idea of deification[4] rather than penal redemption.

The attempt to give the affairs of secular life a divine significance was pioneered by Teilhard de Chardin.[5] It is magnificently illustrated in his account of the exploding of an atomic bomb which he witnessed. With his customary eloquence he described the fears and apprehensions which surrounded the event. The potential for destruction which the explosion was about to demonstrate was on everyone's mind. Was this bomb one day going to show how completely man's technological abilities have outstripped his capacity to control them? Yet, as the earth trembled under the atomic impact and as the sky became incandescent with fire, Teilhard recalled that it was joy, not apprehension, that filled his mind. What he saw in the flecked and shattered sky was not the possibility of destruction but of re-creation. For contained in that mushroom cloud was the

---

of personality which is at the root of these manifestations is similarly called an 'imbalance' (ibid., 10). One wonders if this is adequate. Sin has done much more than simply putting man off-balance. It has knocked him down. He is no longer on his feet. The biblical testimony makes it clear that sin is not only a passive quality such as weakness, inadequacy or deficiency, but also the quality of actively repudiating God's religious and ethical claims upon us. It is this fact which explains the extremely harsh language which Scripture uses to describe it. It is described as adultery, shame, treason, perversion, lawlessness, ungodliness, filthiness, all of which turns us into the enemies of God. See Rom. 1:18–32; 5:6–11; 1 Jn. 3:4; Eph. 4:17–19. Cf. G. C. Berkouwer, The Conflict with Rome, trans. David H. Freeman (Philadelphia: Presbyterian and Reformed Publishing Co., 1958), pp. 76–112.

[4] This theme has long been the domain of Eastern Orthodox theologians. See V. Lossky, The Mystical Theology of the Eastern Church (Cambridge: Allenson, 1957), pp. 9–11, 91–113.

[5] See C. F. Mooney, Teilhard de Chardin and the Mystery of Christ (London: Collins, 1966) and D. G. Jones, Teilhard de Chardin: An Analysis and Assessment (London: Tyndale Press, 1969).

omnipotent and creative power of God which had been un-
locked from the earth.

There are other ways of developing this new relationship
between the natural and the supernatural.[6] As far as the future
is concerned, the most important of these is what is now called
'political theology', an alliance between political Marxism
and religious conviction. A new base has now been established
for political action. If God's saving plan for the earth is being
effected through secular institutions, then political protest and
social revolution are understood as the means God is using to
renovate the world.[7]

These ideas first came to expression in German Protestantism
in Jürgen Moltmann's *The Theology of Hope*.[8] Later, he visited
the United States and published the substance of his lectures.[9]
The revolutionary ideas which are barely discernable in the
first volume become quite evident in the second. His thesis is
simple enough. The ultimate renovation of the earth is the end
to which the Christian subjects all else. This is Christianity's
unifying concept. The means of achieving this renovation is
revolution. And, because it is central to Christian thinking,
the revolutionary means of attaining the goal of renovation
must receive urgent attention. This kind of religious Marxism
moved rapidly from Protestant circles into Roman Catholic
thinking which had been well prepared for its reception by
Vatican II. Johannes Metz has become the chief spokesman
for the Catholic 'political theology' in Germany.

[6] *Cf.* Gregory Baum, *Man Becoming: God in Secular Experience* (New York:
Herder and Herder, 1970).
[7] There is a practical difficulty involved. Revolutions originate on the
extreme right no less than on the extreme left. These two extremes are
anathema to one another. It is clear that those on the political right would
not see God in the midst of a revolution generated by the left, and vice
versa. The problem, then, is in defining what *kind* of revolution God would
identify with.
[8] Jürgen Moltmann, *Theology of Hope: On the Ground and Implications of a
Christian Eschatology*, trans. James Leitch (London: SCM Press, 1967).
[9] Jürgen Moltmann, *Religion, Revolution and the Future*, trans. M. Douglas
Meeks (New York: Scribner, 1969).

What is happening in Germany is by no means of merely parochial concern or peripheral significance. South America, for example, is now ripe for political revolution. The poverty, oppression and thwarted hopes of which revolutions are made abound on that continent. It is not surprising, then, that many South American priests are adopting the stance, if not the practices, of Marxist revolutionaries. What makes this development so significant is that the destruction of the existing order is given messianic significance. The crumbling of buildings, the overthrow of institutions and even the murder of fellow countrymen may be considered signs of God's impending renovation of society.

Revolutions can generate tremendous impetus of their own accord, but allied to religious conviction, they receive a soul, a determination, even an ideology, which they would otherwise lack. This is why the new secular theology cannot be dismissed as merely the brainchild of theologians closeted away in their ivory towers. It may make itself felt one day not only in the lecture room but on the streets of cities smashed by revolutionaries.

Vatican II did not openly sanction revolution, except in one paragraph, but its endorsement of the new eschatology, its giving of sacred meaning to the secular, has opened up the possibility of Church involvement in revolutions. There is no question, though, how radicals in South America will understand that one paragraph which gives tacit approal to revolution:

> By its very nature, private property has a social quality deriving from the law of communal purpose of earthly goods. If this social quality is overlooked, property often becomes an occasion of greed and of serious disturbance.
> In many underdeveloped areas there are large and even gigantic rural estates which are only moderately cultivated or lie completely idle for the sake of profit. At the same time the majority of the people are either without land or have only very small holdings, and there is evident and urgent need to increase land productivity. . . . *insufficiently cultivated estates should be distributed to those who can make these lands fruitful* [my italics].[1]

[1] *Past Con. Church World*, 71.

This, of course, is precisely what happened in the Bolshevik revolution where an economic *élite* were forcibly ejected from the large uncultivated estates which they had owned. At that time the Church was identified with the *status quo*. It supported the imperial order. Now it appears to be identifying with the downtrodden peasant. At least this is how South American theologians like Mendez Arceo and Ivan Illich[2] are interpreting their Catholic commitment. And, in a slightly different context, this is also how the Berrigan brothers are interpreting theirs.[3]

What is alarming about the new direction in which elements of *avant-garde* Catholic thought are moving is not their concern for ethical, social and political matters but the *base* on which the concern is built. Radical priests and some laymen are seeing themselves as the instruments in God's remaking of society and revolution as the way in which this will be achieved. Behind this idea lies the new relationship of the natural and the supernatural. God and the world, as biblically conceived, are no longer at odds with one another, but the supernatural is now merged into the natural. In this search to recover the lost reality of God, to what extent is the left wing of the New Catholicism biblical?

It is doubtful whether progressives can completely substantiate the analysis they have made of traditional belief regarding the natural and supernatural. The distinction between these orders is not spatial as they contend. Rather, there is a hierarchy of being in which there is supremacy of one above another. This supremacy is merely symbolized in spatial terms. Probably the last time anyone thought of reality in terms of a two-layered

[2] Francine du Plessix Gray, *Divine Disobedience: Profiles in Catholic Radicalism* (London: Hamish Hamilton, 1971), pp. 231–322.

[3] *Ibid.*, pp. 45–133. Catholic thinking has changed so dramatically and rapidly in recent years that it now seems hard to believe that Pius IX declared in 1864, with the overwhelming support of the Church, that it was a grievous error to think that 'the Roman Pontiff can, and ought to, reconcile himself to, and agree with, progress, liberalism, and modern civilisation' (Henry Bettenson, ed., *Documents of the Christian Church* (London: Oxford University Press, 1963), p. 384).

cake or even of a three-decker bus was in seventeenth-century
Deism. This is not to deny that elements of Greek philosophy
have found their way into both Roman Catholic and Protestant
thinking on this matter, but the result is rather different from
what some of the recent analyses would lead us to believe.

Certainly Scripture itself does not present reality as separated
layers stacked upon one another. This assertion, of course,
runs counter to Rudolf Bultmann's reading of the New
Testament. He has argued that the early Christians took their
spatial symbols seriously. When Jesus descended into hell, they
believed He really went 'down', and when He arose from the
dead and ascended into heaven, they believed He really went
'up'. That the symbols should be taken seriously is not in
question; what they *mean* is the issue. The ascension in Scripture
is never presented as a space journey. Rather, there is a transition from one order of existence to another, the second order
being supreme over the first. The invisible world into which
Christ entered is basic and primary; the visible world in which
He had lived for thirty-odd years is secondary and derivative
(2 Cor. 4:18). It was this ordering of priorities, among other
things, which was taught by Jesus' ascending upward. To
think that God is isolated in and contained by a sphere of
reality 'above' is simply denied by the New Testament. After
all, the creation is not self-sustaining. It is sustained by God
Himself. Paul draws attention to this fact, citing the Greek
poet Epimenides to the effect that 'in him we live and move
and have our being' (Acts 17:28). God 'is not far from each
one of us' (Acts 17:27) is Paul's conclusion.[4]

But this is only part of the point at issue. What is also at
stake is whether the being of God is in some sense identified
with creation and with secular structures. The teaching of
Scripture seems to be clear on these points too. First, God is not
confused with creation. Creation derives its life from Him, but
there is no community of content between the being of God
and the substance of created life. 'The God who made the

[4] See also Ps. 51:11; Ps. 139:7–10; Is. 57:15; Eph. 2:22 and 4:6.

world and everything in it,' said Paul, 'being Lord of heaven and earth, does not live in shrines made by man, nor is he served by human hands, as though he needed anything, since he himself gives to all men life and breath and everything' (Acts 17:24–25; cf. Is. 42:5). God sustains creation; nevertheless, there is a distance between Creator and creation.

Second, Scripture is also clear that, even if God structures secular reality, its values are not necessarily His. The ethical norms of secular reality constitute what the biblical writers often call 'the world'. Both we and they use this word in a variety of different ways. It is used, for example, of the physical creation, the earth on which we live. It is used, too, in a collective sense. We speak of 'world opinion' or 'the world' passing through a series of political crises. Finally, it is used in a cultural sense to label the network of values which men evolve and by which they live. It should be noticed, however, that although the same word is used both by the biblical writers and our contemporaries, different things are meant. The secular man is largely anthropocentric in his understanding, whereas the Bible is wholly theocentric. The one understands the world largely in relation to himself; the other sees it wholly in relation to God. To the first, the world is important in so far as the interests and desires of men are served by it; to the second, the world is important and meaningful only so far as it is seen in relationship to its Creator.

Consequently, when the Bible speaks of 'the world', it is usually in a cultural and religious sense. It usually denotes that form of life, that network of values, which have been evolved independently of God. Man has attempted to displace God from the centre of the universe and to interpret human significance in this light. The end to which all of life must be directed has become man's own desires rather than the revealed will of God. The secular man, then, is in the Bible's estimate the worldly man.

Christians are said to be in the world and surrounded by a secular environment, but they are not to derive their values

from it (Jn. 17:16). These values can never lead them to a
knowledge of God; they will earn nothing but His condemnation (1 Cor. 1:21, 2:12; Tit. 2:12). Within the secular world
demonic activity is to be found (1 Jn. 5:19). It is for this reason
that James asked indignantly, 'Do you not know that friend-
ship with the world is enmity with God? Therefore whoever
wishes to be a friend of the world makes himself an enemy of
God' (Jas. 4:4; cf. 1:27).

In 1 Corinthians 7:31 Paul states that 'the form of this
world is passing away', thereby adding one more reason for
treating secularity with caution. The word translated as 'form'
(schēma) is full of significance. It has a double meaning: the
outward shape of something or even the clothes someone is
wearing and also something which is fleeting, transient and
changing. The world of secular values, then, is temporary
(cf. 1 Cor. 7:29) and transient. Moreover, its values are merely
outward dressing. And since schēma was also used of the theatre,
the world can even be likened to a play. The scenery is about
to change, and the costumes which are false will soon be
stripped away. Clothed in its present dress of secularity, the
world has no enduring character. The identification of
Christianity with secular life, then, is unwise and unbiblical.
This point has already been made with cogency by Jacques
Maritain.[5]

The whole thrust of the new position lies in its eschatology.
Yet despite this seeming concern with 'end' things, the second
coming of Christ is hardly ever mentioned by the theologians
of the New Catholicism with whom we have been dealing.[6]
Instead, they talk of the emergence of new social structures and
a fresh political order, and identify these with the coming of
Christ's kingdom. The kingdom slowly emerges as society is

[5] Jacques Maritain, *The Peasant of the Garonne: An Old Layman Questions
Himself about the Present Time* (London: Chapman, 1968).
[6] This point is suggested by Bernard Ramm, 'A Critique of the Ethics of the
Theology of Hope', *Towards a Theology for the Future*, eds. David F. Wells
and Clark H. Pinnock (Carol Stream, Illinois: Creation House, 1971),
pp. 189–216.

slowly changed. As these changes occur, Christ can be said to be returning to the earth again – slowly.

An important element of biblical teaching which has been overlooked, however, is the suddenness with which Christ's *parousia* is said to take place. The event will come as unexpectedly as 'a thief in the night' (1 Thes. 5:2; *cf.* Rev. 3: 3 and 16:15), catching many unawares and off-balance (Mt. 25:1–13). Christ's breaking into this world will happen so suddenly as to be completed 'in the twinkling of an eye' (1 Cor. 15:52). This does not really correspond to the idea of the world's giving birth to the cosmic Christ through a long and arduous process of revolution.

Finally, it ought to be observed that there seems to be little recovery of Christian devotional life in the revolutionary side of the New Catholicism despite all the discussion about spiritual renovation. Indeed, some of the new theologians contend that a social concern for man ought to replace personal devotion to Christ. Faith, they say, must be 'deprivatized'.

Scripture, however, does not offer us a choice between loving God and loving our fellow man. Some fundamentalists, it may appear, have acted as if they could love God and ignore the plight of their neighbour; some of the leaders in the New Catholicism have opted for loving their neighbours in the mistaken belief that they are at the same time loving God. Commitment to Christ and love for our neighbour, however, are not mutually exclusive concerns, nor must the latter be confused with the former. According to the great commandment, we are to love God with all our being *and* our neighbour as ourselves; we are to love both God and our neighbour.

And what does it mean to love God? It means to acknowledge Him as creator of the world and the one who continues to give it its life. It means to value life in the terms God does, to make His estimate of the world and of our place in it the measure of what is there, to believe His revelation of Himself in Scripture and to see Christ as the climax to that revelation, as the gift of God to men whose guilt needs to be forgiven and whose sinful condition needs to be changed. Finally, it means to seek God's honour in all our relations with men and with creation, to seek this with all our mind, body, strength and soul.

We are living at an extraordinary moment in Catholic life. Scarcely anyone, even a decade ago, predicted that Catholic thought would change so rapidly or dramatically in the immediate future. But there is today a sense of emancipation in the air. The old system is breaking up; the traditional system of authority is being criticized. Roman Catholics are beginning to say openly that a genuine spiritual life is something they have not always had, but something which they now want.

These changes and the resultant new freedom make a genuine spiritual life not only a possibility but a desperate imperative. In the 1960s, when ideas for reform were in the air, many Roman Catholics experienced a sense of exhilaration. A vital living faith was to be recovered, hope was to be renewed and Christian love was to abound. However, none of this has happened. In a brilliant and sharp critique of these developments, James Hitchcock has shown that precisely the opposite of what was expected has actually taken place.[7] Robust faith, he says, is hardly to be found. Is this surprising when we are told by progressive luminaries like Dewart that the act of theologizing is really the intellectual at prayer and by Eugene Schallert that only a fool thinks he has found God and by William DuBay that the knowledge of God is both inhuman and impossible? Rejuvenation was hoped for, but in many instances disillusionment has come. Faith has given way to doubt, hope to despair and love to a peevish iconoclasm that seems intent only on striking down the Church.

The preceding discussion shows how easily this freedom can be misappropriated. If the theologians of the New Catholicism thought that papal authority was nothing but a form of oppression, it is hard to see how they will fit into the oppression

[7] James Hitchcock, *The Decline and Fall of Radical Catholicism* (New York: Herder and Herder, 1971).

of a Marxist environment. Emancipation in this case has simply led some out of the ways of traditional piety and into those of Marxist–Catholicism. What is plainly needed, then, are some firm principles by which the new freedom will be secured and preserved.

It is quite understandable that some may feel wary of submitting again to an external authority. But history shows clearly that neither reason nor inner experience is the infallible light which it has been thought. Dependence on these flickering sources of illumination will finally issue in a bondage as hard to bear as that from which Catholics feel they have been liberated.

Our situation today finds an interesting echo in a phase of Martin Luther's life. He, too, had begun to find some release from the old system but was frequently overwhelmed by doubts about whether or not his freedom was legitimate. His pivotal treatise, *The Freedom of a Christian*,[8] sets forth his early thinking on this matter. If one reads this work in the light of his other writings from the year 1520, it seems clear that Luther defined freedom in a twofold sense. First, we are free if we are subject to no other authority than that of God's revelation; second, we are free when the gospel of Christ enables us to love God and our fellow men as we ought. Unquestionably, the primary means of freedom is the gospel, and on its trustworthiness Luther stood fast. Thus, in a touching letter to a fellow monk who was similarly troubled, Luther wrote:

Therefore, my dear brother, learn Christ and him crucified. Learn to pray to him and, despairing of yourself, say: 'Thou, Lord Jesus, art my righteousness, but I am thy sin. Thou hast taken upon thyself what is mine and hast given to me what is thine. Thou hast taken upon thyself what thou wast not and hast given to me what I was not.' Beware of aspiring to such purity that you will not wish to be looked upon as a sinner, or to be one. For Christ dwells only in sinners. On this account he descended from heaven, where he dwelt among the righteous, to dwell among sinners. Meditate on

[8] Martin Luther, *Three Treatises* (Philadelphia: Fortress Press, 1960) pp. 262–316.

this love of his and you will see his sweet consolation. For why was it necessary for him to die if we can obtain a good conscience by our works and afflictions? Accordingly you will find peace only in him and only when you despair of yourself and your own works. Besides, you will learn from him that just as he has received you, so he has made your sins his own and has made his righteousness yours.[9]

But if Luther stood fast on the gospel, he also stood fast on Scripture. The one is not known without the other. What is belief if not acceptance of the Bible's account of man's predicament and of Christ's death? What is faith if not committing oneself to the message thus proclaimed through the Bible? Faith does not reside in the Bible; it rests only in Christ. But Christ is savingly mediated only through the biblical word. Thus the objective and subjective sides of belief, credence and commitment cannot and must not be sundered from one another. The preservation of Christian freedom, Luther discovered, depends on being subject to the correct authority no less than in receiving the right gospel.

[9] *Luther: Letters of Spiritual Counsel*, trans. and ed. Theodore G. Tappert in *Library of Christian Classics*, ed. John Baillie, John T. McNeill and Henry P. van Dusen, XVIII (London: SCM Press, 1955), p. 110. The best popular biography of Luther is Roland Bainton's *Here I Stand: A Life of Martin Luther* (New York: Mentor Books, 1950).

5 CHRISTIANITY: A BROAD OR NARROW DEFINITION?

In the Catholicism of an older day, the Church provided the link joining heaven and earth. Both God's blessings to man and man's supplication to God had to pass through this channel. Disappearance of the Church would mean the loss of communication between God and man. Preservation of the Church would guarantee that within a human fellowship, the fellowship of God could also be found.

Evidently, however, the ground has shifted from beneath this concept. A new religious vision is in the making, one in which the presence of God is no longer exclusively contained within the Church. The fellowship of the Church no longer circumscribes the limits within which God can be found. The new theologians are men of universal vision. They see God pervading the whole secular world and man's and God's life blending as both move towards the eschatological end. What place, then, is the Church going to have in the new world?

This may be answered in two ways. First, we must consider how the Church has been affected internally by the new religious vision: what is the new assessment of non-Catholic religion? Second, we must consider how the new vision has affected the Church's external role in national life: how, in more detail, does the new theology view the role of the Catholic Church in world society?

First, how has the Church changed internally? According to the new teaching, man is intrinsically religious.[1] He is *Homo*

[1] This picks up the theme which was central to Protestant Liberalism in its European, British and American expressions. See Reardon's introductory essay in *Liberal Protestantism*, ed. Bernard M. G. Reardon (London: Black,

religiosus as well as *Homo sapiens*. He is the point of integration between the two orders of reality, the point of their structural juncture. The question, then, is how the new view of man can be reconciled with the old view of the Church. More precisely, how can the new theology endorse at the same time the traditional view of the Church (noted for its exclusiveness) and the Teilhardian view of man (noted for its inclusiveness)?

The new thinkers are confident that a reconciliation between the views can be found by reinterpreting the old in terms of the new. In this way, elements of traditional Roman Catholicism are retained even though their real substance has been transformed. At the same time, the new thinkers will be freer in their dialogue with those of non-Christian and even atheistic persuasion. But before looking at the anatomy of this concept, we need to have clearly before us the traditional position which has been adapted and reinterpreted.

The old ideas can be illustrated by an ellipse. It can be said that human religion is arranged in the form of an ellipse with two foci or centres. At the one end of the ellipse is Christ and at the other end is the devil. Every religious view is explicable in terms of the one source or the other. Around the source of light, which is Christ, is gathered the Roman Church. Around the other source, the source of darkness, is gathered everyone else including Protestants. There are, it is true, gradations (in kind no less than in degree) to both sources. For example, atheists are evidently most clearly identified with the devil, non-Christian religion which is at least theistic is less so and Protestantism is even further from this source of darkness. Nevertheless, the whole of non-Catholic religion, despite its differences and its degrees of darkness, is excluded from the circle of Christ's presence. Similarly, there are differences in nearness to Christ within the Catholic Church. The practice of canonizing saints is a way of saying that certain people have

1968), pp. 9–66. Rahner was near the truth when he called Küng a Liberal Protestant. But what Rahner apparently had not realized is that Küng could, with equal justification, reciprocate in kind.

lived nearer to Christ than others. And there are still others on the fringes of Catholicism, by contrast, who show very little evidence of their Christward relation.

Nevertheless, the important point is this: despite differing relations to the two respective sources, the presence of Christ is exclusively contained within the Roman Catholic Church and, with few exceptions, those not within Catholicism are not related to Christ. No matter how many beliefs a Protestant may share with a Catholic, he is still excluded from the presence of God until he has entered the Roman Church. There is only one body of Christ and that is the Catholic Church. 'She cannot admit,' says Karl Adam firmly, 'that men can be saved by membership in other societies established by the side of and in antagonism to the primary Church of Humanity founded by Christ.'[2]

The reasoning behind this position is well presented in this important volume of German theologian Karl Adam. There are two steps in the argument. First, the truth of Christ, he asserts, is by nature exclusive. The sayings of Christ, such as the claim that He is the way, truth and life and that no-one can enter into relation with the Father except through Him, cannot be overlooked or casually dismissed. Adam's first point here is entirely right. If the idea of antithesis is lost, if truth and error, right and wrong, become indistinguishable from one another, then Christianity will have ceased to exist. Christianity's whole premise is that it is the true revelation of God which always stands over against other religion. Whereas other religion is always a human mythology in one form or another, Christianity unfolds the truth about God and man. It is the only genuine yardstick by which the worlds of material and spiritual reality can be measured.

The second step in the argument, however, is the one which has given traditional Roman Catholicism its distinctive doctrine of the Church and one which makes Protestants

[2] Karl Adam, *The Spirit of Catholicism*, trans. Justin McCann (New York: Image Books, 1963), p. 169.

uneasy. Traditional Catholicism maintained that the connect-
ing link between man and Christ is the Church, whereas the
Reformers, for example, argued that it is faith. This does not
mean that the Reformers held a weak view of the Church. Both
Luther and Calvin insisted that the Church had a vital part
to play in bringing faith to birth. Luther went as far as endorsing a doctrine of baptismal regeneration, and Calvin was at ease
with the old dictum that if you would have God for your
Father, you must have the Church for your Mother. Nevertheless, the Reformers did entertain a distinctive view of faith.
The gospel was received through faith rather than through any
mechanical means in the Church. This position was contested
by Roman theologians of the day who established an identification between Christ and the Catholic Church. With few
exceptions, they said, man can only know Christ through this
Church. Since there is an exclusiveness in Christ's teaching
about Himself, so there must be an exclusiveness in the Church's
teaching about herself. If Christ is the only source of truth,
then joining the Catholic Church is the only way of finding that
truth.

> The one Christ and the one Body of Christ belong indissolubly
> together. He who rejects the one true Church is all too easily
> brought, as by an inexorable logic, to go astray also about Christ.
> As a matter of fact the history of revolt from the Church is at the
> same time a history of the progressive decomposition of the
> primitive faith in Christ.[3]

This position was deftly summarized in the third century by
the north African bishop Cyprian and officially endorsed by
the Fourth Lateran Council (AD 1213) in the dictum that
'Outside the Church there is no salvation' (*Extra ecclesiam nulla
salus*).[4]

Today, however, in an intriguing new development, Roman
Catholic theologians themselves are trying to pierce the armour
of this argument. It is vulnerable, they say, in its claim that

[3] *Ibid.*, p. 173.
[4] Cyprian, *Ep.*, LXXIII, 21.

there is an air-tight relationship between Christ and the
Catholic Church.

The old argument was formulated by men who thought they
could know God's truth infallibly. Their confidence, it is said,
was the child of classical logic in which truth was always truth,
error was always error and the distinction between them was
never blurred. The classical mind was composed of black and
white only, never of grey. Consequently, there was for traditional Catholics an unbridgeable chasm between Christ and the
devil, light and darkness, Catholic and non-Catholic religion.
But is this not, it is asked, a rather facile oversimplification of
the real situation?

On the level of cognition – what man can know – the old
Catholic was confident and affirmative. The new Catholic, by
contrast, tends to be agnostic in some respects and uncertain
in others. He is the child of the existential, not the classical,
world. For him, the object of religious knowledge, in this case
Christ, is often obscure. The sharp lines of distinction in matters
of truth are now untenable, perhaps even undesirable. The
concern has shifted from objective definition to subjective
experience. It is not *what* you believe which is important but
that you believe, not what you believe *in* but the quality of your
commitment *as* you believe.[5]

Consequently, some people have begun to wonder – rather

[5] In the modern period, Søren Kierkegaard is credited with effecting the
transition from external assent to internal commitment. Against the Hegelian-
ism of his day, he insisted that 'truth is subjectivity'. The difficulty implicit
in this position is elucidated by Clark: 'If there is no objective truth, if the
How supersedes the What, then can truth be distinguished from fancy?
Would not a suffering Satan be as true as a suffering Saviour? . . . If there
were objective knowledge about Christianity and other objects, an individual
could judge the quality of his passion on the basis of its objective reference;
but if God and perchance the devil also are hidden, and if one is limited to
the subjective, passionate appropriation, there would seem to be no distin-
guishable difference between the truth of God and the truth of Satan'
(Gordon Clark, *Thales to Dewey: A History of Philosophy* (Boston: Houghton,
Mifflin, 1957), p. 489). Whether Clark's criticism is applicable to Kierkegaard is debatable, but it is a valid warning against the danger into which
existentialism may lead.

loudly as it turns out – whether there is a distinction to be made between truth as it exists in itself and truth as it is understood in the Church. Do we ever understand truth as it really is? Does not our fallible humanity always interpose itself like an obfuscating filter between the truth and what we understand about that truth?[6] If this distinction can be maintained, then truth could mean different things for God and for man. Reality for God is utterly perspicuous; for man it is always blurred. To God, truth is always an integrated whole; for man, it usually appears as fragmented insights which, at some later point, might have to be revised. Truth is absolute to God; it is relative to man.

A good illustration of the new view of truth, although it is only one of many which could be used, is the book entitled *God, Jesus and the Spirit*.[7] This book, says its editor Daniel Callahan, was made necessary by the new spirit which Vatican II encouraged. It has forced Roman Catholics to rethink their faith in non-traditional terms. Callahan, therefore, commissioned a number of authors to re-examine the doctrine of God, the meaning of Jesus and the place of the Spirit in Christian life. The three subjects which were chosen would suggest that what was really in view was the doctrine of the Trinity, but Callahan denies this. Modern theologians, he says, no longer think of truth as a whole, nor do they think of Christianity as a system in which doctrines are inter-related. Rather, truth is fragmentary, and Christian theology is made up of a series of partial and unrelated insights. Themes are taken up *seriatim*; their interconnections are not examined.

If this position can be sustained, there is little doubt that the

[6] In theology, the precise relationship between God's truth and man's understanding of it has been debated for centuries. But even if they are not precisely identical (univocal), it has always been assumed that there are elements of continuity between them (analogical). They are not totally dissimilar (equivocal). For a discussion of the issues involved, see Baptista Mondin, *The Principle of Analogy in Protestant and Catholic Theology* (The Hague: M. Nijhoff, 1963).

[7] Daniel J. Callahan, ed., *God, Jesus and the Spirit* (London: Chapman, 1969).

air-tight relationship between Christ and the Church has been broken. The truth of Christ may be absolute, but the Church can never see it clearly enough to comprehend it absolutely. Her doctrinal formulations can never be more than *approximations* to the truth. Some are good approximations, others are bad, but all are subject to revision. Since the Church can no longer declare with that old ring of authority what the truth is, she must accordingly abandon her old claim to be in exclusive possession of it.

This line of reasoning has an unusual history. For about twenty years before Vatican II, Catholic thinkers – especially those in France – had been probing this distinction, to the acute discomfort of traditionalists. In his opening speech to the Council, Pope John apparently alluded favourably to these ideas. However, we should note that it is one thing for theologians to speculate about truth like this, but quite another for the Pope to do so. Indeed, in the brief interim between the reading of his speech and its appearance in official translation, one traditionalist at least went on record as saying that the Pope could not possibly have endorsed these ideas.[8] To the conservatives' chagrin, however, it turned out that he had, for he said that 'the substance of the ancient doctrine of the deposit of faith is one thing, and the way in which it is presented is another'.[9]

To a Protestant casually browsing over the speech, this sentence may appear so bland as to seem almost meaningless. It may seem as if John was merely saying that each generation must re-express the unchanging core of Christian truth in its own language and jargon. But this idea is so obvious the Pope need not have said it, and it is certainly not capable of precipitating the furore which followed his statement. We must look elsewhere for its real significance. In the audience of trained theologians, John could use a kind of theological shorthand

[8] See Antoine Wenger, *Vatican II: Première Session* (Paris: Centurion, 1963), pp. 46–50.
[9] Abbott, p. 715.

which would be interpreted in the way he wished. His single sentence was a pithy, if deceptively simple, summary of the new ideas: there is a distinction to be drawn between truth in itself ('the deposit of faith is one thing') and truth as it is comprehended by the Church and taught to the world ('the way in which it is presented is another').

This distinction is primarily responsible for freeing contemporary Roman Catholicism from its traditional attitudes towards culture and religion. Because the close relationship between Christ and the Church has been broken, no doctrinal formulation from the past can bind Catholic attitudes in the present. Each formulation is to some extent deficient. Each generation must try afresh to penetrate the deposit of faith more deeply and correspondingly reformulate its own faith. No generation will again be able to claim eternal and unchanging status for its formulations.

Hans Küng was the first major theologian to pursue these ideas in print. For example, he tried to give Council decisions a merely local or momentary significance.[1] They were infallible in the moment in which they were enunciated, but at a later date they could be changed. But then in 1970, he moved to a more logically satisfying position in his book *Infallible? An Inquiry* in which he denied that infallibility can ever be found in any form or in any place (including the Vatican).

The New Catholicism, then, does not find itself limited by past statements on man's religion. The traditionalists were formulating faith for their time; progressives are now doing it for ours. Both parties are said to be working with the same 'deposit of faith', but as they work with it, they see different things.

---

[1] *Cf.* Küng's statement, for example, that 'the decisions of the Council of Trent (or of other councils) cannot be regarded as binding definitions where they concern questions which are being put differently today in the light of completely different problems. . . . No council is granted a fresh revelation; its solutions are tied to the capacities of the theology of its time' (Hans Küng, *The Church*, trans. Ray and Rosaleen Ockenden (London: Burns and Oates, 1967), p. 419).

According to progressives, the crucial statement in the Council documents occurred early in the Constitution on the Church. There it is stated that 'at all times and among every people, God has given welcome to whosoever fears Him and does what is right'.[2] This sentence appears before any of the discussion on the traditional means of salvation, such as the sacraments. This order is important, as Butler explains:

> The constitution on the Church . . . in its chapter on the People of God, opens its discussion of salvation by a primary affirmation that 'whosoever fears God and does what is right is acceptable to God' (n. 9). Only after laying down this principle does it proceed to teach that the objective means of salvation are given by God in the People of God, that is the Church. This inversion of the traditional order of thought may be taken as a shift in emphasis from objective to subjective. Salvation is, for the individual, radically dependent on subjective good intention [rather] than on external ecclesiastical allegiance.[3]

If salvation now depends on internal attitude rather than external allegiance, then it can be found without the Church's help. Salvation can be enjoyed outside the Church and independently of it. But what is to be done with the old dictum, *extra ecclesiam nulla salus*? Butler, for one, has decided to reinterpret it rather than dispense with it. The Council's new position, he says, means that in men of all religions as well as in in men of no religion, 'Christ is (anonymously) at work and . . . in them, the Church *extra quam nulla salus*, is transcending her own visible limits.'[4]

Roman Catholics have been uneasy with the old dictum for some time, and certain well-defined exceptions to it have always been allowed. Some years prior to the Council, for example, the Church refused to allow Father Feeney in Boston a rigid interpretation of this formula. Indeed, Feeney was

---

[2] *Con. Church*, 9. One of the French theologians who did so much to influence the Church towards many of the new positions is Henri de Lubac. On this particular point see his *Catholicism: Christ and the Common Destiny of Man*, trans. Lancelot C. Sheppard (London: Burns and Oates, 1950), pp. 107–126.

[3] Butler, *The Theology of Vatican II*, p. 167.

[4] *Ibid.*, p. 126.

finally excommunicated for refusing to allow that any outside
Rome could be saved. But despite this growing tendency to put
the traditional past in a softer light, Butler's statement comes
as an abrupt innovation. If the limits of the Church are coextensive with the limits of mankind, then there is no more point
to saying that there is no salvation outside the Church than
there is to arguing that only human beings can be saved. Hans
Küng has said that the twisting of old formulations in this way
is, as he put it, 'downright equivocation'. It would be better
to dispense with the formula than try to manipulate it as
progressives sometimes do.

In the new view, then, how is Christ related to mankind?
The best illustration here is not an ellipse, but a series of
concentric circles. At the centre of all the circles is Christ.[5]
Moving outward, each circle which is further from the centre
exhibits less of Christ's reality and is correspondingly less
Christian in its consciousness.

The innermost circle, which is gathered around Christ, is
comprised of the Roman Catholic Church. Catholics are said
to be 'incorporated' in Christ[6] in a full embodiment.[7] They
sustain the closest relationship to Christ. However, His reality
is said only to 'subsist' in the Church, and this, in the subtle
language of conciliar theology, implies that He is also to be
found outside the Roman Church; that is, His reality also
transcends the first circle.

The second circle is made up of non-Catholic Christians.
They are not incorporated in Christ as Roman Catholics are
but then they are not, as traditionalists used to claim, totally
alienated from Him either. They are said to be 'linked' to Him,[8]

[5] It will be noticed that one of the original sources, namely the devil, seems
to have disappeared. References to judgment or purgatory in the Council
documents are extremely scarce and never elaborated beyond brief quota-
tions mainly from Scripture. It is difficult to know what is intended by these
references. Perhaps their inclusion was made principally on account of the
conservatives' evident discomfort with the prevailing universalism.

[6] Con. Church, 11, 14, 31.

[7] Con. Church, 8; Dec. Ecumenism, 4.

[8] Con. Church, 15.

implying some form of relation but not one as real or as genuine as that enjoyed by Catholics. Just because non-Catholic Christians are separated from Rome, they are not automatically separated from Christ. They are not alienated from truth; they are only separated from its fullness.

The third circle is composed of non-Christian religions. It would be too much to say that they are either incorporated in Christ or joined to Him. Nevertheless, even Jews, Hindus and Moslems are not entirely without Christ's light. They are 'related' to Him.[9] The assumption that there are gradations in proximity to Christ and varying degrees to membership in the People of God caused the Council to be wholly positive in its assessment of non-Christian religion.[1] All religions bear some marks of being touched by Christ, however much this inner truth may be overlaid by outward error. The Council sought to recognize areas where there was agreement between the teaching of the Catholic Church and that of other religions and to ascribe the community of content to both their common source – Christ.

The Council was not saying that all religions are equally true. Rather, it was trying to combine the old idea that Christ is to be found only in the Roman Church with the newer idea that something of the divine is to be seen in all men. There was the merging of a vision which is universal in scope with a concern which is Roman in particularism. The outstanding problem which has been posed, but hardly answered, by the new concept is how much of a Christward orientation is needed to establish membership in the People of God. Some theologians, building on the Council's teaching, have argued that one day the People of God will become coextensive with the human race.[2] Are all, then, implicitly members of God's kingdom even now?

[9] *Ibid.*, 16.
[1] *Decl. Non-Christian Religions*, 2–4. The best explication of the Council's thought at this point is *Les relations de l'Église avec les religions non-Chrétiennes*, ed. A. M. Henry (Paris: Cerf, 1966).
[2] *Cf.* 'This People is becoming the eschatological, universal People of God

The final circle is made up of atheists. But even atheists are not wholly devoid of a Christward relation. Among them are what Rahner has called 'anonymous Christians'. This is a disturbing conception – for the traditionally-minded at least – because it has always been assumed that such 'anonymity' destroys faith. To be sure, the Council does not endorse atheism in any of its forms. The Church, it said, 'sorrowfully but firmly' repudiates atheism because its doctrines are contrary to both 'reason' and the 'common experience' of mankind.[3] But it is interesting to note that, although the Council rejected atheism, it refused to pronounce any more anathemas on it. Why?

In the texts[4] on atheism, two basic shifts in understanding have evidently taken place. First, the Council did not think that atheism is, of necessity, morally wrong, whereas traditionally an atheist has always been looked on as both stupid and wicked. Says Karl Rahner:

> This . . . is implied in the reference to the fact that, on the one hand, there exists an explicit atheism, which is widespread socially and held to be self-evident in all simplicity, while on the other hand, general Christian principles do not entitle us simply to condemn such atheists as being gravely guilty before God.[5]

Second, the Council did not exclude the possibility of an atheist's being saved. Philosophical atheism and an inarticulate Christianity may cohabit in the same man at the same time. Consciously and explicitly he may be an atheist; unconsciously and implicitly he may be a Christian. This conclusion can be drawn when two of the Council's texts are placed alongside one another.[6] The two passages read as follows:

---

composed of all the nations of the world' (Rudolph Schnackenburg and Jacques Dupont, 'The Church as the People of God', *Concilium*, I, No. 1, January 1965, pp. 34–35).

[3] *Past. Con. Church World*, 21.

[4] *Con. Church*, 16; *Dec. Bishops*, 11, 13; *Dec. Priests*, 4; *Past. Con. Church World*, 19–21.

[5] Karl Rahner, 'The Teaching of the Second Vatican Council on Atheism', *Concilium*, 3, No. 3, March 1967, pp. 9–10.

[6] Apparently it was the Council's intention that this should take place, for a footnote on the second passage refers the reader back to the first one.

Those also can attain to everlasting salvation who through no fault of their own do not know the gospel of Christ or His Church, yet sincerely seek God and, moved by grace, strive by their deeds to do His will as it is known to them through the dictates of conscience. . . .[7]

All this [sharing in Christ's resurrection] holds true not only for Christians, but for all men of good will in whose hearts grace works in an unseen way. For, since Christ died for all men, and since the ultimate vocation of man is in fact one, and divine, we ought to believe that the Holy Spirit in a manner known only to God offers to every man the possibility of being associated with this paschal mystery.[8]

The first passage is usually understood to include atheism in its reference. Like other men, atheists do not know 'the gospel of Christ' and sometimes not even 'His Church'. But, like others, they can also 'attain to everlasting salvation'. How? The answer is provided in the second passage. There we learn that atheists have the same ultimate destination as others. Christ died for them also and as a result, atheists already share in His resurrection, evidenced by the fact that in them, too, 'grace works in an unseen way'. Beneath the façade of atheism, then, the eye of faith sees the Spirit's work and Christ's saving grace. A man may be outwardly and explicitly atheistic but he may well be inwardly and implicitly Christian. And it needs to be remembered that his standing before God depends on the interior dimension rather than the exterior façade. Rahner sums up accordingly:

All these texts obviously do not assume that these atheists will become *explicit* theists within their own understanding before they die, and that they will be saved *because* of this. If this were so, these texts would simply state the truism that an atheist can be saved when and insofar as he ceases to be an atheist. Such an interpretation would deprive the texts of any serious meaning, hardly worth a conciliar pronouncement.[9]

This approach to atheism falls within the context of the new approach to man as a whole. First, it assumes that all men are

[7] *Con. Church*, 16.
[8] *Past. Con. Church World*, 22.
[9] Rahner, 'The Teaching . . .', p. 12.

implicitly religious and that Christ is the explanation of this. Second, it sees man's religion in terms of grey, and rarely ever in terms of black and white. Third, it also fits into the new sacred-secular relationship, which offers some under-girding to the 'political theology' which has given parts of Roman Catholicism a Marxist appearance. Finally, the new assessment of atheism dispenses with the necessity of the Church for salvation, and this accords with the general mood of the New Catholicism. The *raison d'être* for the Church has now disappeared, in effect making salvation dependent not on external Church allegiance but on internal self-commitment. Even those who see some future for the institutional Church concede that in the decade ahead, Catholicism will be much changed.[1]

Our second question concerns the role of the Church in world society.[2] How will the Teilhardian vision affect the Church in its outward relations? If we can judge from the Church's thinking in the recent past, it seems clear that the role which Rome has enjoyed in world affairs in the past might be modified significantly. Perhaps the outstanding characteristic of the Council's teaching on the Church's place in national life was its vagueness:

> This conciliar program is but a general one in several of its parts –
> and deliberately so, given the immense variety of situations and
> forms of human culture in the world. Indeed, while it presents
> teaching already accepted in the Church, the program will have
> to be further pursued and amplified, since it often deals with
> matters in a constant state of development.[3]

Actually, the options which were open to the Council in the matters considered remain clear and unchanged. What seems to be 'in a constant state of development' is not so much

[1] *Cf.* Charles Davis, *A Question of Conscience* (London: Hodder, 1967), pp. 181–239; Karl Rahner, *The Christian of the Future*, trans. W. J. O'Hara (London: Search Press, 1967); Michael de la Bedoyère, *The Future of Catholic Christianity* (Philadelphia: Lippincott, 1966) and Jeremiah Newman, *Change and the Catholic Church* (Dublin: Helicon, 1965).
[2] See *Past. Con. Church World*, 63–76.
[3] *Ibid.*, 91.

political and economic theory as the mind of modern Catholicism. It was this fact which caused the Council to culture a somewhat uncommitted outlook. The Church wants to retrench its role; more particularly, it wants to eliminate the idea that it is a world force directed from its headquarters in Rome.

At any rate, the Council seemed to hold itself aloof from the world's political forces. Communism and capitalism, for example, were both condemned because both lead to materialism.[4] On the other hand, aspects of both systems were also commended. The right to own private property and to be free from absolute control by the state was conceded to the West. Equally important for the Communist countries[5] was the denial of the profit motive on which capitalist systems operate:

> The fundamental purpose of this productivity must not be the mere multiplication of products. It must not be profit or domination. Rather, it must be the service of man, and indeed of the whole man, viewed in terms of his material needs and the demands of his intellectual, moral, spiritual and religious life.[6]

Yet on the crucial issue of how and to what extent the state should control the economy, the Council was ambiguous.[7] However wise or unwise this ambivalent position may be, it does represent a marked departure from the days when Rome openly told countries how to govern themselves politically and economically. It leaves open the possibility, too, that Catholicism could work out different political alliances in different countries. To some extent this has been practised for some time. In the early years of the Vietnam war, for example, Pope Paul reflected the European outlook when he condemned the war effort while many American bishops reflected mainline

[4] *Ibid.*, 63.
[5] This is an interesting development in view of Rome's previous hostility to Communism. In 1931, for example, Pius XI observed that 'Communism teaches the fiercest warfare between classes. . . . It shrinks from nothing in the pursuit of its aims . . . and when it seizes power it displays incredible cruelty and inhumanity. . . . Its open enmity to Holy Church and to God Himself is, also, all too clearly proved by its actions . . .' (Bettenson, p. 393).
[6] *Past. Con. Church World*, 64.
[7] *Ibid.*, 65.

American feeling, as it was then, that this war was in a good cause. The diverse opinion was simply a pragmatic adjustment of Catholic policy to different situations. Now, however, the adjustment is also theoretical.

The vagueness of the Council's discussion, then, is important not for what it says but for what it does not say. There was a time when the Church regulated the life of its members in minute detail. Jaroslav Pelikan, the Yale historian, has noted this, saying of the past that:

> The Roman Catholic is trained to look to his church not only for guidance and inspiration, but also for direction on how to live, how to work, and how to think. Even in a complex modern society the long arm of the Church's power reaches into almost every province of his life. The main course of his Friday dinner; the neckline of his wife's evening gown on Saturday night; the movie he attends on Sunday afternoon; the school to which he sends his children on Monday morning; the labor union or service club he wants to join; his attendance at the wedding or funeral of a Protestant friend – these are only some of the questions on which the church has spoken and on which the church expects its authority to be obeyed.[8]

This tight regulation is no longer true. The Church is now pulling back. With the emphasis shifting so rapidly from the older concern with outward Church authority to the newer one of the Spirit's inward control, the Roman Catholic hierarchy now shows little willingness to issue edicts which might be ignored by the average Catholic. This process of retraction is reversing nearly eighteen centuries of accumulated tradition in the Roman Church. It is about as unCatholic as the Reformation was. Psychologically, for many Catholics, it is one of the most shattering developments ever to have taken place. Theologically, it is one of the most important because the main element in the structure of Catholicism, the doctrine of the Church, has been significantly modified. The future is now wide open.

[8] Jaroslav Pelikan, *The Riddle of Roman Catholicism: Its History, Its Beliefs, Its Future* (New York: Abingdon, 1959), p. 92.

The disintegration of institutional Catholicism may lead to a form of belief which is less sympathetic to biblical belief than was traditional Catholicism. But it is possible that other developments could follow. The breakdown in the structure of the Church and in the Pope's authority is accomplishing, by dint of circumstance, what the Reformers tried to do by force and argument. As they saw it, the essentials of Christianity had been lost in Rome's all-enveloping doctrine of the Church. Faith was defined as assent to what the *Church* taught; salvation consisted in receiving the sacraments which the *Church* offered; Christianity had become identified with what the *Church* was. In each case, the Church assumed a primary role that should only have been secondary.

For the Reformers, Christianity was not identical with the Church. The Church was not an end in itself; it was only a means to an end. The end which it should have served was the spiritual life of its members, the corporate life of their fellowship. When the Church lost sight of its essentially pastoral and subservient role, it lost sight of its biblical mandate. And when this happened, the power of the Church grew at the expense of genuine Christianity. The confusion between ends and means in regard to the Church was really what the Reformation was all about.

The present situation, in which the structure of the Church is showing some cracks, is latent with possibility. Words of Martin Luther, spoken in the sixteenth century, do not seem as scandalous to Catholics now as they might have then and because they honour Christ, they are really not scandalous at all:

> I pray the God of all mercies that he teach Your Grace this one thing, that Christ and his Word are more, higher, greater, and more trustworthy than a hundred thousand holy fathers, councils, churches, popes, etc., for the Scriptures call all of these sinners and lost sheep. Be bold, therefore, and do not fear the rulers of the earth. Christ is greater than all devils and more to be feared than princes.[9]

[9] Luther, *Letters of Spiritual Counsel*, p. 164.

6 THE CHURCH:
THE PEOPLE OR THE POPE?

The struggle over authority in the Roman Catholic Church is the most tangible evidence of the power which the New Catholicism has acquired. Many contemporary Catholics are opposed to the traditional pattern of papal control. The Pope, however, cannot change. Reconciliation between the old and the new in the Church would involve serious compromise for both sides and is out of the question, granted the present terms of the debate.

It is easy to see how the Church arrived at this position. The traditional view of authority was part of a tightly integrated world of thought. Ecclesiastical authority rested naturally and comfortably in this world. God had committed His work of salvation to the Church and had left the Pope, His representative on earth, to direct it. To know God one had to belong to the Church, and to obey God one had to heed His representative.[1]

For the Catholic today, however, the close identification between God and the Church is, as we have seen, less certain. Those who are not in the Church are not necessarily separated from Him. God is 'in' the world, not isolated 'above' it. The

---

[1] In the early Church, the pressure of heresy did as much as anything to create this view. Thus, at the beginning of the second century, Ignatius wrote that all should 'follow the bishop as Jesus Christ followed the Father' (Ignatius, *Ep. Smyrn.*, viii). A similar pressure, that of schism, forced Cyprian in the mid-third century to argue that 'the bishop is in the Church and the Church is the bishop, and if any one be not with the bishop he is not in the Church . . .' (Cyprian, *Ep.*, LXVI, 7). These two representative views give us useful information on some of the causes which led to the emergence of an authoritative figure in the Roman Church. No such figure, of course, existed for at least the first three centuries in the Church's history.

secular is tinged by the sacred; God is found to some extent in all men. If this is all true, if salvation can indeed be found outside the Church, then the traditional role of the Church in the world has been seriously affected. It is this process of decentralization which Karl Rahner has in mind when he speaks of the contemporary '*diaspora*'.[2]

The implications of decentralization are potentially dangerous for the Church's authority. The traditional power structure has been built up around the Vatican. It depends on centralization. Can the Pope still rule when the Church is busy decentralizing itself? This question has recurred with nagging persistence in every post-Vatican II crisis in the Roman Church.

Decentralization does not mean that the majority of contemporary Catholics no longer believe in authority or Church government. What is at issue is not whether there should be authority in the Church but what kind it should be. The argument is over two different theories of authority, two different conceptions of how the Church should be governed, two different world views in which the Church plays entirely different roles. The conflict is not only between doctrines, but also between mentalities and ideologies.

What are the two conceptions and wherein lies their incompatibility? The one theory, it can be said, uses a 'descending' form of authority, the other an 'ascending' form.[3] The first is traditional, the second progressive. Traditionalists think of the Church as if it were a pyramid whose apex is the Pope.

[2] In New Testament times, this word was used of those Jews who, as a result either of past deportation or of voluntary emigration, settled outside Palestine. It was asked of Jesus, 'Whither shall this man go that we shall not find him? Will he go to the *diaspora* among the Gentiles?' (Jn. 7:35). It is used in a contemporary setting of those who have emigrated from the confines of traditional Catholic faith. Sometimes they have even broken their ties with the Church but not, it is argued, with Christianity. The analogy is not apt. Jews outside of Palestine were intensely loyal to Judaism, retained the law and the prophets, observed all the feasts and paid their religious tax. Catholics in *diaspora* today are not always loyal to the Roman faith and rarely ever observe its feasts.

[3] *Cf.* Walter Ullmann, *A History of Political Thought: The Middle Ages* (Harmondsworth: Penguin, 1965), pp. 12–44.

He governs all who are 'below' him; the movement of
authority is from the top downward. The progressives' view
is entirely different. For them, the Church is a more or less
flat plane. There is little thought of elevation one above another
in the hierarchial structure. The movement of authority, if there
is movement, is from the bottom. Authority should begin, they
say, not with the Pope, but with all the people. When the
Spirit reveals His mind to the people and they reach a
consensus, the Pope is then obligated to articulate this
corporate view and put it into doctrinal form. A statement
produced in this way is authoritative, not because the Pope
has proclaimed it, but because he has acted on behalf of the
people, articulating what was believed by a majority of them.

The practice of this theory of authority, however, sometimes
involves difficulties. For example, William DuBay maintained
this view and then discovered, to his chagrin, that the people did
not always see matters the way William DuBay thought they
ought to. He was left with only two alternatives: either he would
have to change his view of authority or he would have to leave
the Church. Since the first was unthinkable for him, he opted
for the second. The dilemma in which he found himself could
be seen in germinal form even in his study, *The Human Church*.[4]

The progressive who holds the 'ascending' view of authority
and then finds that the people as a whole do not believe what
he believes about a given matter is confronted by more than
an intellectual problem. For, on the basis of the progressives'
own definition, the Pope should heed the views of the laity
because in and through them the Spirit is manifesting God's
will. It is no less serious for a progressive theologian to be out
of accord with the Spirit than it is for the Pope, although
progressives have not always realized this. Those who have,
like Charles Davis, inevitably leave the Church.[5] And if these
progressive and traditional views of ecclesiastical authority
continue, a certain paralysis may be expected in the Church's

---

[4] William DuBay, *The Human Church* (London: Muller, 1967).
[5] Charles Davis, *A Question of Conscience* (London: Hodder, 1967).

functioning, and a steady trickle of progressive priests will probably continue to leave the Church.[6]

In the century which divides Vatican I (1870) from Vatican II (1962–65), much has happened in Roman Catholic thinking. This is particularly true as the Church has pondered the basic question of authority. Vatican I produced a clear statement on the 'descending' form of authority. In places, Vatican II produced its antidote in the 'ascending' form of authority, although it did also endorse the traditional ideas. The First Vatican Council, then, gives us a useful gauge against which the significance of the new ideas can be measured.

Historically, the reunification of Italy, completed in 1870, meant that the Pope had been effectively deprived of temporal power in Europe.[7] Once, popes had asserted their authority over most of Europe and even attempted to seat and unseat kings. They were able to deny salvation to whole nations. But in time, the Pope's temporal sovereignty was finally restricted to a tiny state in Rome known as the Vatican. But if the Pope's temporal power had been severely restricted, his spiritual power, by contrast, seemed to increase. By 1870, Pius IX felt the time was ripe to promulgate the idea of papal infallibility. The Pope's infallibility in matters of doctrine and ethics had been widely believed for centuries. But prior to 1870, it had not received the status of dogma. Even Luther had made reference to it and, on one occasion, scandalized his audience by insisting that neither popes nor councils are infallibly preserved from error in doctrinal matters.

The Constitution on the Church from Vatican I localizes almost all powers and authority in the Pope who, accordingly, rules all those 'below' him in the hierarchical structure. This

---

[6] See J. Drane, *Authority and Institution: A Study in Church Crisis* (New York: Bruce Publishing Co., 1969) and C. O'Grady, *Church in Catholic Theology: Dialogue with Karl Barth* (London: Chapman, 1969).

[7] The best account of these years from a Catholic perspective is that of E. E. Y. Hales, *Catholic Church in the Modern World* (New York: Doubleday, 1958). It should, however, be checked against J. B. Bury, *History of the Papacy in the Nineteenth Century* (New York: Schocken Books, 1964).

fact emerges in the chapter headings of the constitution: 'Of
the Institution of the Apostolic Primacy in Blessed Peter', 'On
the Perpetuity of the Primacy of Blessed Peter in the Roman
Pontiffs', 'On the Power and Nature of the Primacy of the
Roman Pontiffs' and 'Concerning the Infallible Magisterium
of the Roman Pontiff'. The Constitution purports to deal with
the Church, but it has concerned itself only with the Pope! The
Pope's attitude to the Church, Catholic radicals complained,
could be summed up in one sentence: 'L'Église, c'est moi!'

It seems clear from Vatican I that at this time the Pope was
not under any great obligation to consult the Church before
making authoritative statements. He spoke on his own authority
and not necessarily as the representative of the people. It is
true, as Küng is anxious to point out, that papal power has
never been entirely arbitrary. The Pope could never define
doctrines that would go against natural law or commonly
accepted Christian morality or previously defined dogmas.
But this does not mean that he had to consult the Church
before pronouncing on matters concerning faith or morals.
Indeed, the idea of consultation which came to the fore at
Vatican II in the form of collegiality, was deliberately eliminated from the Constitution at Vatican I, where a proposal
much along the lines of Vatican II's collegiality came on to
the council floor. This formula stated:

> The Pope, though as an individual person and acting of himself he
> can err in faith; nevertheless, *using the counsel and seeking the help of
> the universal Church* [my italics] . . . he cannot err.[8]

The final text on infallibility omitted the idea of 'using the
counsel and seeking the help of the Church'[9] because it suggest-

[8] Cuthbert Butler, *The Vatican Council: The Story Told from Inside in Bishop
Ullathorne's Letters, II* (London: Longmans, 1930), p. 95.
[9] The text reads as follows: 'We [*i.e.*, Pope Pius IX] . . . teach and define
as a dogma divinely revealed: That the Roman Pontiff, when he speaks *ex
cathedra* . . . is endowed with that infallibility, with which the Divine
Redeemer has willed that His Church – in defining doctrine concerning
faith or morals – should be equipped: And therefore, that such definitions
of the Roman Pontiff of themselves – *and not by virtue of the consent of the Church*
[my italics] – are irreformable' (Bettenson, p. 385).

ed that the Pope might be dependent on the Church, and this was quite incompatible with the idea of his ruling from 'above'.

When we move to the corresponding Constitution on the Church from Vatican II, it may appear at first sight that the same conception of papal power and authority has survived intact. The Council of Florence said the Pope's power was 'full', the Council of Trent added that it was 'supreme', Vatican I went further and said it was 'universal' and Vatican II recapitulated the whole tradition saying that the Pope has 'full, supreme, and universal power over the Church'.[1] His authority after Vatican II seems as absolute and unchallenged as before. But is this the case?

The Council, as we have already seen, was not averse to endorsing mutually exclusive theologies. Sometimes this was the only way the opposing factions would allow a document to see the light of day. So the presence of this 'descending' conception of authority in the Constitution does not *ipso facto* exclude the presence of the opposite view. And when it is remembered that in recent years the traditional view has become something of a *bête noire* to progressives, it seems most likely that they would at least insure that it was neutralized, if not undermined by their own conception. This happened in four discernible ways.

First, the order and composition of the Constitution on the Church was designed to emphasize the importance of the people and to de-emphasize the importance of the Pope. Only one out of eight chapters says anything about the Pope as compared with all four from Vatican I. Even then, the Council came to deal with papal authority only after it had dealt with the people in two preceding chapters. The implication is that authority is rooted in the people, not derived from the Pope. Commenting on the Constitution's order, Yves Congar says that it means that 'the first value is not organization, mediatorial functions, or authority (all aspects of the "descending" conception) but the Christian life itself and being a disciple' (the

[1] *Con. Church*, 22.

essence of the 'ascending' conception).[2] The attention has been
shifted from the outer Church structure to the inner realm of
religious experience, from an authority derived from ecclesiastical position to one built on subjective 'insight'.

Second, in a subtle way the progressives sought to qualify
even that sentence which gives the Pope his traditional powers.
Alongside the first sentence which states that he has 'full,
supreme, and universal power over the Church' is a sentence
which apparently takes all these powers away! It says that he
'can always exercise this power freely'.[3] At first sight this
sentence would seem to strengthen and add to the statement
which precedes it, but it should be clear by now that first
glances are seldom reliable when interpreting official Catholic
documents. This sentence has a hidden thrust, as Butler
explains: 'The word translated "can" is *valet*. It appears to
mean that when the Pope so acts [with consultation] his action
is "valid". It does not, in that case, imply that the Pope is
morally justified in acting without due consultation.'[4] The
Pope can exercise full, supreme, and universal power *validly*
only when he consults the Church and speaks on its behalf. If
he exercises his power independently of the Church, he is
acting invalidly. Indeed, his action is without moral justification. So once again, traditional wording has been turned around
to serve rather liberal ends. The juxtaposition of these two
sentences makes it quite clear that the issue of consultation is
the exposed nerve in the whole debate.

The third challenge which the progressives mounted is even
more serious and could paralyse the Church in its traditional
functioning. The idea of papal infallibility could not be denied,
but the progressives did succeed in neutralizing it by introducing two other forms of infallibility in the Church whose joint
action would be more than enough to counteract any assertion

[2] Yves Congar, 'The People of God', *Vatican II: An Interfaith Appraisal*,
pp. 199–200.
[3] *Con. Church*, 22.
[4] Butler, *The Theology of Vatican II*, p. 105.

of papal power. First, all Catholics in whom the Spirit's light is shed have an infallible perception of truth (*sensus fidei*).[5] Progressives argue that their concern over the *sensus fidei* is traditional rather than innovative. They are not departing from the truth, they say, but affirming it. This is no doubt correct. The Church has always believed in the *sensus fidei*. The main difference between its past and its present affirmation, however, is that formerly the magisterium had the task of interpreting truth, whereas now the Church at large is doing so. Second, in addition to the infallibility of all Catholics is the infallibility which all the bishops possess and which is peculiar to their office. Both these infallibilities were said to be the direct result of the one Word of God (by which is probably meant the inner religious perception which the Spirit gives).

Theoretically, of course, this triumvirate of infallibilities in the people, bishops and Pope should always act in concert, serving the same end. But what happens if they do not? What should the average Catholic do if the Pope should offer some infallible teaching which a Catholic's religious insight should lead him to repudiate with equal infallibility? On whose side should the bishops infallibly align themselves? This is, to be sure, a nightmarish situation, but it is not wholly alien to our Church situation today. It is becoming increasingly clear, especially after the birth-control *débâcle*, that the Pope can enforce only that teaching in the Church which the Church is willing to receive.

It seems clear that today's layman no longer feels the same awe and respect for his teachers that he used to.[6] He has now emerged as a force to be reckoned with. For the first time in conciliar history, a special document on the laity was approved, thus redressing the imbalance of an exaggerated clericalism which traditional ideas have fostered. For the first time in the

[5] See *Con. Church*, 12, 35; *Past. Con. Church World*, 52.
[6] One of the best essays on this theme is by E. Schillebeeckx, 'Un Nouveau Type de Laic', *La Nouvelle Image de l'Église*, ed. Bernard Lambert (Paris: Maine, 1967). The gist of it, however, can be found in less polished form in his *The Layman in the Church* (New York: Alba House, 1963), pp. 7–34.

history of the Roman Church, laity are threatening to assume
the role of the magisterium. Never before has it been said that
every Church member possesses the Spirit[7] and that he has,
therefore, direct access to the fountains of Christian truth. It
has always been thought that this access was the private
preserve of the Church's official teachers.

Indeed, in traditional thinking, the Church consisted of two
halves: 'the teaching Church' and 'the learning Church'.
Since the Church's authoritative teaching body alone had
access to religious truth, it therefore had the obligation of
unfolding it to the rest of the Church. And 'the learning Church'
had the responsibility of receiving and believing this teaching.
There was no room for the latter body to question or doubt the
teaching offered by the former. To question the teaching of
the magisterium was to alienate oneself from the supply of
truth.

But with the new teaching that every Christian has the Spirit
and has direct access to the truth, the traditional functioning
of the magisterium has been seriously qualified. Since every
Catholic has the means of discerning truth, he has become
part of 'the teaching Church'. And insofar as he heeds what
he sees, he also belongs to 'the learning Church'. 'It seems
possible,' Butler says, 'that, in fact, the whole Church is, under
different and correlative aspects, both *docens* [teaching] and
discens [learning].'[8] And since the Spirit gives to even the
lowliest and humblest a religious perception which is infallible,
there seems little doubt that the teaching roles of the magisterium and even of the Pope are, to some extent, being changed.
These changes, in effect, neutralize the Pope's absolute infallibility. Now the progressives went to work on the Pope's
absolute power and sought to administer the *coup de grâce*.

As a final challenge, they attempted to eliminate independent papal action by reasserting what they think is the genuinely

---

[7] See Hans Küng, 'The Charismatic Structure of the Church', *Concilium*,
4, No. 1, April 1965, pp. 23–33. *Con. Church*, 20–22.
[8] Butler, *The Theology of Vatican II*, p. 110.

'traditional' view – that the Pope is subservient to the bishops. Their view became evident in the decision on collegiality. Jesus, it is argued, first gave authority to all the apostles (the college) before singling Peter out to be their spokesman. In a sense, the apostles were members of a committee whose chairman was Peter. It was Peter's role to guide the discussion and then articulate the decision when the vote was taken. Certainly, it is said, Jesus did not in any way separate Peter from the other bishops or elevate him over them.

Progressives then apply this principle to the present situation. Bishops have succeeded the apostles, not merely because they have come after them in time, but because the apostles are now said to live on in the bishops. Consequently, apostolic power and authority have been reincarnated in the episcopal office. The same pattern of functioning which pertained among the apostles must also pertain among the bishops. Jesus has not chosen the Pope to be separate from or elevated above the other bishops. Rather, the Pope is the chairman of the committee. He announces the corporate decision, but at no time does his individual authority outrank that of any other committee member. The Pope, in other words, is not free to make independent authoritative pronouncements. He merely has the role of a spokesman, announcing the opinion of a majority of bishops. His authority, then, is valid only when he speaks after due consultation with them.

The Council's teaching on collegiality was an attempt at qualifying the Pope's power. Independent papal action would be eliminated, it was hoped. To put the matter the other way around, the bishops of the Church hoped that in the future they would control what was offered as authoritative teaching. Indeed, some progressives turned the whole matter into a moral and doctrinal issue of the greatest importance. Butler, for example, claimed that 'a pope who attempted to define an article of faith without use of such means (of consultation) would commit a grievous sin'.[9] Not only would the Pope

⁹ *Ibid.*, p. 105.

become a sinner, Küng continued, but in these circumstances
he would place himself in schism. 'The Pope cannot by any
means define arbitrarily or against the will of the Church as
a whole; the Pope himself has to be on his guard against
schism.'[1] Küng did not need to add that schism is usually
punished by excommunication and, in fact, canon law allows
for the Pope's deposition should he go into heresy or schism.
Put in this way, the stakes which are involved in collegiality
are high, but, of course, not every progressive has wanted to
state the problem in this way.

The progressives' fourfold attempt at locating authority in
the people rather than the Pope and at replacing the 'descending' form of authority by an 'ascending' form was too successful
to be ignored. Indeed, Pope Paul responded in a way that may
subsequently bring discredit on his office. What really alarmed
him was the notion that his authority was not separate from
that of any other bishop. He decided to append a Note to the
Constitution on the Church which would explain the real
meaning of the passages by which he felt he was threatened.
The Note was added after the Council had completed its work
on the Constitution, so no vote was taken and no official
comment was made.

The Explanatory Note denies, against the whole teaching
on collegiality, that there is 'any *equality* between the head and
the member of the college'.[2] The Pope, it continues, 'proceeds
according to his own discretion . . . in structuring, promoting,
and endorsing any exercise of collegiality.'[3] So the Pope is,
after all, independent of the other bishops. He can choose in
which role he wants to speak. If collegial action coincides
with his own opinions, then he can, as head of the college of
bishops, articulate their views which are also his. But if
agreement does not exist, then he can move into another role,
that of 'Shepherd of the Universal Church', in which he can

---

[1] Küng, *The Living Church*, pp. 301–302.
[2] *Con. Church Addenda*, 1.
[3] *Ibid.*, 3.

act without any reference to the bishops. He can disregard their views or change them as they are implemented. The reverse, however, was ruled out. He may act without the bishops, but they may never act without him.

Now, how do these relationships work out in practice? The most agonizing problem which the Roman Church has had to confront in its post-Vatican II days has been birth control. It was obviously not an issue which could be kept on the back burner indefinitely since millions of Catholic families were intimately involved in it. Tradition demanded that the illegality of practising birth control be affirmed, but a majority in the Church wanted a more flexible approach to the matter. Paul agonized over the problem for some months and then, without reference to the bishops, came down on the side of tradition. Should he have called a meeting of bishops to resolve the issue by collegial action? If the Constitution on the Church is read with the aid of the Explanatory Note, the answer is in the negative. As Shepherd of the Universal Church, the Pope has sole responsibility for the well-being of his flock and can issue teaching on his own authority. But if the Constitution is read as the Council intended it to be, then he should have resolved the issue by collegial action. When the bishops eventually got together in Rome after Pope Paul's encyclical had been issued, they took him to task for not consulting them. Leo Suenens, the Belgian cardinal and leader of the progressives, was most forthright in this matter, letting the Pope know that he had acted unconstitutionally. Whether this was so, of course, depends on how the document is interpreted. There are two ways of looking at it. From one perspective, Pope Paul acted quite within his power, while from the other perspective, he did not.

Until Vatican III can resolve ambiguities like this in one way or another, the possibilities for confusion in the Church remain. Confusion of this kind, however, does have the effect of vitiating traditional authority. But even if the Pope does use his traditional powers to rule the Church, the Church can still move in the opposite direction with a measure of legitimacy under the Spirit's leading.

Two points of comment naturally arise out of the preceding discussion. First, it seems evident that the concept of the 'people' is both ill-defined and ill-conceived. Who constitutes this people is never clarified; the whole human race may implicitly constitute it even if this is not explicitly evident yet. But it is also possible that this people can be identified properly only with an *élite* within Roman Catholicism. It is not unusual to find an assumed apostolic consciousness among some of the *avant-garde*, and there is always a corresponding irritation when the Church does not recognize their prophetic insights. Under such circumstances, the pattern of subsequent action is now well established: the prophet departs from the Church and writes a scandalous account of his persecution by the authorities.

Fixing the exact limits of the people of God is vitally important for progressive theologians for it is through this people that the Spirit will speak. Is the Marxist philosopher, Herbert Marcuse, to be considered in or out, and, correspondingly, is his 'message' the word of God for our times or is it not? Is the Spirit addressing the Church through the secular radicals like Callahan and Novak, or is the Spirit to be identified only with those who have left Roman Catholicism? Or does he associate only with the lowly and despised and not with theologians at all? Until the people-concept is clarified, its use in attempting to check the Pope's authority will be nothing more than a piece of demagoguery.

Second, it should be noted that underlying some of the progressive antipathy to traditional authority is not merely an appreciation for democracy but also a scepticism about the infallible possession of truth in any form. Hans Küng, in his *Infallible? An Inquiry*, has localized the problem in the claim that infallibility is dependent on propositions. Küng is not against giving faith a clear, definitive statement, which he sees as having occurred in Scripture itself. But he is against identifying that propositional definition as truth. Language is always fluid, he says; its meanings change and, besides, it is quite incapable of explaining or describing divine realities. The desire to equate the truth of God with written dogmatic statements – on which papal infallibility depends – is a concession, says Küng, to the error of identifying faith with certainty. In his opinion, the biblical authors did not make this mistake, and we should not either. Their writings are merely the response to, the after-reflection on, their religious experience. What is important is the experience, not their account of it.

For Küng, God alone is infallible. The word infallible can be used of no-one else (including the Pope) and nothing else (including Scripture). Religious certainty is to be found, therefore, not in the hearing of Scripture, nor in obedience to the Pope, but in an encounter with the infallible Christ. Just how this experience can be said to be infallible and so to induce certainty is, however, far from clear. The Christ who is preached arises out of documents which Küng frankly says are defective. In order to know Christ's true nature, the person who is seeking this obscured Christ has to have some infallible discernment. Alternatively, he is forced back on to the promise that God will guide the Church into all truth, and therefore in the act of his hearing, the Christ-message will, for him, become true even if it began as false in the preacher's mind.

Without realizing it, Küng has either enlarged the idea of infallibility – making it necessary for everyone to be infallible – or he is asking for a leap of faith which is frankly incredible. He is asking the Church to believe that every time Christ is preached from the defective biblical documents, a miracle occurs so that a genuine rather than a defective Christ emerges to confront the hearer. One may have real sympathy for Küng's contention that infallible popes and councils have made errors again and again, but the best solution is to repudiate false infallibilities, not the concept of infallibility itself. Given careful definition in relation to the biblical documents, infallibility is something which Christians in all ages have maintained.

The future of Roman Catholicism depends on the outcome of the struggle between the people and the Pope. It can be said that what is in conflict is two world-views, two ideologies, two different conceptions of the Church. The one position finds it difficult to introduce changes into official teaching; the other finds it difficult not to. The first is legally entrenched in the Church; the second is popularly entrenched. What is going to happen, we are tempted to ask, when the immovable traditional object is met by the irresistible progressive force?

Perhaps the conflict will never reach incendiary proportions, and maybe the constitution of the parties in debate may change. With the passage of time, the most radical may leave the Church, the most conservative may die and the laity may repudiate its more liberal suitors. The Roman Church would then be able to pursue effectively the policy which Pope Paul evidently wants for it now: a respectful hold on traditional faith, an openness to a moderately progressive outlook and a radical approach to social problems. If Pope Paul lags behind progressives in their theology, they often lag behind him in his liberal political and social views. Only time will tell whether such a *via media* will be possible. But even if it is, the theology of the Counter-Reformation will not again be an option. That the future will see a progressive Catholic theology is not really in debate; what is undecided is only *how* progressive it will be.

7 INTO TOMORROW

The task of interpreting the Roman Catholic mind is difficult. Cardinal Newman once remarked that 'none but the *Scola Theologorum* is competent to determine the force of Papal and Synodal utterances, and the exact interpretation of them is a work of time'.[1] But even with the passage of time, nuances and implications still elude the most diligent analysts, especially if they are Protestant. Despite this, at least the main lines of the new Catholic theology seem clear, and they are certainly quite different from those of traditional orthodoxy. Says Gregory Baum:

> A conservative outlook on the magisterium and the conservative claim that church teaching never changes simply cannot explain what happened at Vatican II. After all, at that council, the Catholic Church, formally, solemnly, and after a considerable conflict, changed her mind on a number of significant issues.[2]

This change of mind in matters as important and fundamental as revelation, the relation of the natural and supernatural, salvation and the doctrines of the Church and papal authority has rendered the vast majority of Protestant analyses of Catholic doctrine obsolete.[3] It has also placed on Protestants an obligation to revise their thinking about Rome.

[1] John Henry Newman, 'Letter to His Grace the Duke of Norfolk', *Newman and Gladstone: The Vatican Decrees*, ed. Alvan Ryan (Notre Dame: U. of Notre Dame Press, 1962), p. 76.
[2] Gregory Baum, 'Liberalism Lives in Theologians', *St. Louis Review*, 23 October 1970, p. 3.
[3] If Protestants are still in doubt about the change of mind, they should compare the systematic theologies current at the turn of the century and those in use now. See, for example, A. Tanquery's *Manual of Dogmatic Theology*, trans. John T. Byrnes (New York: Desclee, 1959), which represents the high-water mark of nineteenth-century orthodoxy, and the contemporary

The importance of these changes, as well as our obligation
in the face of them, inevitably leads us to ask what the Church
will be like in 1980. With such a volatile situation and with so
many unknown factors, predicting the Church's future becomes
a hazardous business. Besides, from the time of Balaam, those
who have engaged in professional prophesying have always
laid themselves open to suspicion! These difficulties notwithstanding, we will attempt some predictions, if only that we might
see magnified in the future what is at present only germinal.
It will at least help us measure the significance of the current
developments.

The pivot on which the future turns would seem to be the
shift towards subjective religious experience and away from
objective Church allegiance. This emphasis will mean that
two men may regard each other as Catholics, not because both
adhere to the same (objective) teaching but because both
appear to share the same (subjective) experience. In an
existential age, *how* you believe is far more important than *what*
you believe.

The Council has recognized the distinction between truth
in itself and truth as it is comprehended by man. This distinction is made necessary by the way in which man is influenced
by his culture. His background and upbringing, his education
and occupation all condition him to 'see' truth in a certain way.
This conditioning explains why he can never comprehend
God's truth in its utter purity.

Some time in the decade ahead, therefore, it may become
impossible to speak any longer of *the* Catholic faith as a whole,
since it will mean different things to different men in different
places. The significance of the term may become purely local.
We will perhaps speak of the Catholic faith in Southern Ireland
and of the Catholic faith in France. In a land as diverse as the

---

manual by Johannes Hofinger and Francis J. Buckley, *The Good News and
Its Proclamation: Post Vatican II Edition of the Art of Teaching Christian Doctrine*
(Notre Dame: U. of Notre Dame Press, 1968). These two books represent
two entirely different worlds.

United States, we may even have a number of different types of Catholicism.

To a certain extent this cultural differentiation has always been the case. In the last three decades at least, the French have become famous for a certain kind of mystical spirituality, Americans have usually had a trace of pragmatic activism in their veins and the Irish have often tended to define the faith in terms north of the border. But what I am suggesting here is that in the future the Roman Catholic Church may no longer think of herself as Catholic or universal in the old sense and, furthermore, that this change will be brought about not primarily for pragmatic, but for theological, reasons.

So far, the Church has tried to adjust herself to the realities of cultural influence on the formation of faith by acknowledging, for example, the use of the vernacular in worship. This has been a pragmatic change. However, future diversity may occur as the Church acknowledges the insufficiency of her grasp on truth. And this is a theological matter. When truth becomes less distinct, when the sharp lines which traditional theologians drew become blurred, the Church is correspondingly forced to be less comprehensive in its proclamation and teaching. This theological shift is consonant with the general shift in emphasis from the objective ecclesiastical teaching to the subjective religious disposition.

When the magisterium begins to speak on a narrow front, the individual will have far more latitude and freedom to shape his own belief. Once this latitute is granted, environmental factors will more and more intrude into and exercise an influence upon emergent Catholic faith. This does not mean that total disintegration will follow. There is a certain homogeneity to cultures, to national identity and even to familial life, and these influences will probably aid the local Church in preserving unity and cohesion. But, the intrusion of these factors on the shaping of Catholic belief will mean that, in the old sense and on the traditional basis, the unity of the Church will disappear.

It follows, of course, that the office of the Pope will be reduced to that of a moderator over a mass of largely independent local churches. In the modern world, monarchies are under assault, and the papacy, in so far as it is an ecclesiastical monarchy, will not escape the scythe of its critics. Where modern-day monarchies have survived, they usually remain only in symbolic form with all of their effective powers removed. If this pattern is duplicated in the case of the Pope, he will retain his titles, but all of his former power will be transferred to local churches. They will govern themselves in the light of their own religious insight even if they politely doff their hats to Rome.

A second key development as far as the future is concerned is the new religious vision which is in the making. The theoretical developments have already taken place in the new dialogue between belief and non-belief; the future will be shaped by their translation into practice.

How will this be worked out? Three possibilities seem to stand out. First, we could see an accelerated exodus from the Church. If salvation is radically dependent on subjective attitude rather than on the acceptance of objective teaching, then the role of the Church will become considerably less significant. Those who find that its strictures cramp their style or limit their freedom will be tempted, as they were not in the past, to leave the Church and go into '*diaspora*'. If many Catholics really leave, it will be a tragic irony. Progressives have consistently argued that the Church will prove attractive to secular men only if it refines and to some extent alters many of its traditional ideas. But traditionalists have complained that if this altering takes place, the Catholic's birthright will have been bartered for a mess of secular pottage. The future might prove the traditionalists correct.

The second possibility which should be considered for the future is the unification of Protestant and Catholic Churches, perhaps under the umbrella of the World Council of Churches.

The relation of the Roman Catholic Church to the Ecumenical movement, whose beginning is usually dated from the

Edinburgh Conference of 1910, has been a rather complex affair. In general, Rome has shown itself unwilling to participate in the movement, although in recent years it has softened its stance on this matter.[4] But we should remember that the union of all Christians was a long-range goal which was in the back of Pope John's mind when he called the Second Vatican Council. John's order of priorities demanded that Catholics set their own house in order before entering into negotiations about unity. This was also the order of priorities set out in Hans Küng's *The Council, Reform and Reunion*.[5]

We should note, however, that many of the obstacles which formerly stood in the way of union have now disappeared. On many matters, a fruitful exchange is now considered possible, whereas formerly it was not. For example, the question of Scripture is now proving to be a unifying rather than a divisive factor. The looser stance which many Catholics have adopted has brought them closer to non-traditional Protestantism. The encyclical *Divino Afflante Spiritu* of 1943, that sanctioned moderate biblical criticism, and the endorsement of its teaching by the Council has opened the way for a cross-fertilization of ideas. Then again, by cutting salvation loose from membership in the Church, Rome has established the possibility of direct discussions which need not degenerate into proselytism, since Protestants need not become Catholics to be saved. Behind this development is the less dogmatic assertion of truth and the willingness to allow subjective experience to be pivotal in determining religious postures. These attitudes are already present among many of the Protestants in the ecumenical movement.

Other encouragements to union might be mentioned. Papal authority has always been a hindrance to unity, but this is now

[4] See Oliver Tomkins, 'The Roman Catholic Church and the Ecumenical Movement, 1910–1948', *A History of the Ecumenical Movement, 1517–1948*, ed. Ruth Rouse and Stephen Neill (Philadelphia: Westminster, 1968), pp. 677–696.
[5] Hans Küng, *The Council, Reform and Reunion*, trans. Cecily Hastings (New York: Sheed and Ward, 1962).

under criticism within the Roman Church itself. The Catholic priesthood in the past has been so different from its Protestant counterpart that a working union seemed unthinkable. In recent years, however, Protestantism has shown a marked interest in liturgical as well as sacramental worship. Catholics, on the other hand, are developing new approaches to worship which bring them nearer to traditional Protestant liturgical worship. The legitimacy of some of the practices which were formerly difficulties, such as clerical celibacy, are being carefully reviewed. Catholics are showing far more interest in the origins of Christianity, particularly in the biblical and patristic eras, and some Protestants seem to be showing a growing appreciation for tradition.

These movements and ideas may be harbingers of greater things to come. In the face of this, it is important for those concerned with the preservation of apostolic Christianity not to make the wrong point. All too often the idea of Christian unity has been criticized as if biblical Christianity had no interest in it. No-one can read the New Testament and still retain this conclusion. Many of its letters were written with the precise intention of *preserving* Christian unity when it was threatened by false teaching or false practice. The New Testament writers are unequivocally in favour of Christian unity provided it is established on a Christian basis. That is to say, Christians must find their unity in the same *truth* which they profess rather than in some common project in which they all participate. Furthermore, the truth they profess must reiterate the truth which the apostles taught. This is the apostolic succession which the New Testament teaches.

The desire for unity and the possiblity of its realization are not, then, necessarily wrong. In fact, the fear of unity is a fairly recent development in traditional Protestantism. Harold Rowdon has shown that the Edinburgh Conference of 1910 was really fathered by evangelical Protestants.[6] All through

[6] Harold H. Rowdon, 'Edinburgh 1910, Evangelicals and the Ecumenical Movement', *Vox Evangelica*, 5, 1967, 49–71.

the nineteenth century, the cause of Christian unity was almost
completely the cause of evangelicals. Only subsequently did
others become interested in it. And, some time after 1910,
because of the interest of those from other theological persua-
sions, the ecumenical movement was abandoned by the
evangelicals. Now traditional Protestants wish it would die.
The chances of its dying, however, are slight.

What needs to be analysed carefully, then, is the basis for
any further union. First, will the basis be theological rather
than practical? Second, if the basis is theological, will it also
be biblical? Does the union commend the biblical gospel or
does it obscure it? These criteria should be kept in mind as the
future unfolds.

The third possible development is the emergence of a Marxist-
oriented Catholicism, especially in some areas of South America.
It is conceivable that Catholic commitment could provide the
soul for a series of revolutions which would be interpreted as
God's action in renovating and restoring broken society. To
be sure, the Catholic *avant-garde* is not the only one interested
in the theology of revolution. According to Marty and
Peerman's *New Theology No. 6*, the annual index to what is going
on in theology, revolution and its related issues was the theme
which dominated theology as a whole in 1969. Granted, in
recent years, theologians have not been of one mind. Some
have argued for the legitimacy of violence and others for the
necessity of non-violence, some for revolution and others for
peace. Nevertheless, there is a significant element which is
oriented in the Marxist direction, and some Roman Catholic
thinkers are among these.

But, even if future 'evangelism' is not politically militant, it
will have a different objective than at present. Its purpose will
not be to proclaim a Church-related salvation; rather, it will
seek to focus more precisely what all men see in a blurred way
already. Thus, its purpose will really be didactic rather than
evangelistic. To sum up, it would appear that Catholicism is
presently moving away from both Christian particularism and

Roman centralization and moving towards religious univers-
ality and ecclesiastical independence.

A final possibility, which runs counter to the developments
discussed above, should be considered. Many traditional
Protestants have been optimistic that, as a result of the post-
Vatican II struggle, many Catholics will belatedly acknowledge that historical Protestant belief holds the key to their
religious needs. The doctrine of the Church, which was a
principal bone of contention at the Reformation, is now being
modified in a decidedly Protestant direction. Other reasons
cited for this optimism are the new concern with Scripture and
the new concern over glossolalia.

On the matter of Scripture, there can be no question at all
that the Catholic Church has changed her attitude, if not her
mind. In teaching that sermons should be more biblical and
that priests should meditate more on Scripture, the Council
certainly emphasized something which has pleased traditional
Protestantism. How much one can deduce from this change,
however, is questionable. It is true that many lay people today
are being confronted by biblical teaching in a way they never
were in the past. Significant and even dramatic results may
follow. On the other hand, the attitude towards Scripture
which the New Catholicism has taken could well nullify the
good intentions of going back to Scripture. After all, Protestantism as a whole has always disclaimed tradition as a revelatory
source and, in so far as it has an authoritative Word, finds it in
or in conjunction with Scripture. The availability of Scripture
and the widespread deference to it in Protestant circles has not
guaranteed a return to historic belief. It seems naïve, therefore,
to assume that, on the basis of a wide availability of Scripture
in Catholicism and a rising interest in its teaching, the outcome
will necessarily vindicate traditional Protestant belief.

The new concern over speaking in tongues, especially as it
has manifested itself in Roman Catholic circles, is also seen
as a sign that genuine Christianity is being rediscovered in
Catholicism. This may be, but it does not follow irresistibly

from the facts. There are some, of course, who have made glossolalic phenomena the touchstone of Christian authenticity. In
their view, the simple fact that Catholics now speak in tongues is
prima facie evidence that a recovering of Christian reality is in
progress. There are, however, other possible interpretations,
and the fact that the Ranaghans teach that this experience is
valid for those on both the theological 'left' and 'right' should
alert us to the fact that all is not well in every case. Indeed, in
view of the new and dramatic Catholic interest in subjective
experience, something like the glossolalic phenomena was to
be expected anyway. What has to be decided, therefore, is
whether or not this concern is an outgrowth and consequence
of a recovery of biblical Christianity. This decision is considerably more complex than some imagine, and the difficulties
involved should warn enthusiasts against becoming too
euphoric as they look into the future.

Both Protestants and Catholics are heirs to an enormous
accumulation of polemical writing, originating from both sides
of the religious question. Our mutual past cannot be ignored,
but it must not be allowed to distort our mind in regard to the
present. There are aspects of the centuries-old argument in
which we might not wish to be implicated and which we may
well regret. Certainly, our object in discussion must never be
that of simply defending the old position, be it Catholic or
Protestant. On the Protestant side, at least, the Reformers
would be the first to say that their opinions must not be looked
on as if they constituted divine revelation. Rather, Protestants
today should seek, as they always sought, to subject all human
opinion to the teaching of Scripture.

This is a theological task for which Paul has set brief but
important guidelines in Ephesians 4:15: '. . . speaking the
truth in love'. Neither aspect of the injunction should be
compromised. Biblical truth cannot be watered down;
Christian character must not be violated. It must be in *love*
that we speak the *truth*. 'Inflexible in the essentials of biblical
faith, flexible in its non-essentials and charitable in all things'

is a dictum we would do well to enforce on ourselves. Our discussions must always rise above the level of stale or petty polemics. Love must direct us to the point where the biblical Christ is confronted, for truth will only be found here. And it is the truth question alone which must absorb our attention. This is, after all, what theology is all about.

It is easy to forget that the Church is not ours, but Christ's. He purchased it by His death (Acts 20:28) and He has guaranteed to preserve it through the centuries (Mt. 16:18). That there is still Christian faith in the world speaks of God's providence; that we can still expect God's continued blessing speaks of His grace. As we look into tomorrow, then, our hope rests not in ourselves but in Him who said, 'All authority in heaven and on earth has been given to me. . . . I am with you always, to the close of the age' (Mt. 28:18–20).

APPENDIX

MARY: AN UNRESOLVED PROBLEM

The Roman Catholic doctrine of Mary has become difficult for Protestants to accept. Here, it seems, is a set of beliefs and practices which have developed with insufficient regard for the teaching of the canonical Scriptures. Aware of the discomfort this teaching causes in Protestant circles, the Council was faced 'with a serious, indeed an agonizing, problem and dilemma'.[1] This was so for two reasons.

First, the Council was trying to minimize the differences between Protestantism and Catholicism, and Mariology is one of the most outstanding differences. Should the Council, therefore, dilute its teaching at this point to accommodate Protestant feeling? Or should the Church remain true to its traditional teaching even at the expense of alienating the non-Catholics she is seeking to woo? Second, the Council was concerned to return to the original sources for Christianity, and Catholics have usually admitted that Scripture knows nothing of a developed Mary devotion.[2] Should the Council trim its beliefs in accord with Scripture or should it retain traditional teaching

[1] Butler, *Theology of Vatican II*, p. 84.
[2] 'At the end of the fourth century,' writes Daniel-Rops, 'Mary's two fundamental characteristics, her divine maternity and her perpetual virginity were part of accepted doctrine' (Henri Daniel-Rops, *The Book of Mary*, trans. Alastair Guinan (New York: Hawthorn Books, 1960), p. 87). At this time Mary devotion became systematized and the regular feasts in her honour established. But how much earlier can we go? Daniel-Rops does claim that 'her image can be found on the walls of the catacombs where she is often pictured as a young mother holding her child' (*ibid.*, p. 91), but this does not establish that Mary devotion existed. T. J. Shahan's review of this phenomenon in his *The Blessed Virgin in the Catacombs* has simply led him to claim that Mary adoration is first clearly established at the end of the second century. Certainly, it is unknown in Scripture.

at the expense of the desire to return to the biblical writers? The Council's solution at this point was not quite as ingenious as in other matters, but it still gave the impression of achieving some of these mutually exclusive objects. On the one hand, the substance of traditional teaching was retained (for Catholics) but its importance was underplayed (for Protestants).[3] At the same time, little appeal was made to extrabiblical sources in establishing the traditional Marian doctrine.

The Council said that it was not giving 'a complete doctrine on Mary'.[4] Despite the disclaimer, what follows in the main section on Mary is a fairly complete summary of the traditional doctrine.

Mary, it is stated, was predestined to her role as Mother of God. In fact, God 'willed [that] the consent of the predestined should precede the Incarnation'.[5] When the consent was obtained, Mary was able to assume her co-operative role in bearing God. She is, the Council says, 'acknowledged and honoured as being truly the Mother of God and Mother of the Redeemer'.[6]

God's predestination of Mary conferred on her a certain dignity. Tradition has always said, and the Council agreed, that this dignity implied her possession of a fullness of grace by which her divine mission was accomplished.[7] It is said her fullness of grace was assumed by the angelic greeting in Luke 1:28. Thus, traditionally, Mary has been said to possess

[3] This is evident in the decision to include the section on Mary in the Constitution on the Church rather than having it as a separate document. In this way, it is suggested that Mary, despite all her privileges, is still only a member of the Church rather than some transcendent being separated from the ordinary company of sinners.

[4] *Con. Church*, 54

[5] *Ibid.*, 56.   [6] *Ibid.*, 53.

[7] Of all creatures, Mary alone according to Catholic teaching can say to one of the members of the Trinity, 'Thou art my son, this day did I beget thee' (Ps. 2:7). 'From this fact of her maternal relationship with the Eternal Word of God, came her predestination to that relationship from all eternity and the consequent fullness of grace and privilege that made her worthy to be the Mother of God' (Anselm Burke, *Mary: In History, In Faith and In Devotion* (New York: Scapular Press, 1956), p. 86). *Cf. Con. Church*, 56.

natural and supernatural gifts which other people never have.[8] Grace, it has been taught, left in her a repository of knowledge which was able to preserve her from sin. The Council endorsed this.[9] Such a state seems to imply that Mary did not have to contend with original sin, and so the belief about her immaculate conception came to a cogent form quite early in the Church's life. It was reaffirmed at Vatican II.[1] Like Christ, Mary was conceived without sin, she triumphed over it in her life and, to complete the process of identification, she also ascended into heaven. This latter belief, which was finally promulgated as a dogma in 1950, was also endorsed by the Council.[2] The climax to the development is the claim, which emerged early in Church life and is restated by the Council, that Mary is the New Eve who, by her obedience, reversed the ill consequences brought on by the first Eve's disobedience.[3] To sum up, Mary's unique experience of grace preserved her from original sin (immaculate conception) and from sinning during her life. Her body was never impaired (perpetual virginity), nor did

[8] Pope Pius IX in his *Ineffabilis Deus* commented on the angelic greeting thus: 'This solemn and unparalleled salutation, heard at no other time, shows the Mother of God as the seat of all divine graces, and as adorned with all the gifts of the divine graces, and as adorned with all the gifts of the divine Spirit.' *Cf. Con. Church*, 63.

[9] The Council of Trent declared of Mary that she was able to 'avoid all sins, even those that are venial' on account of a 'special privilege from God'. *Dec. Just.*, XVI, 23. *Cf. Con. Church*, 58.

[1] This belief which has been held for many centuries was dogmatically defined in 1854 in these words: 'at the first moment of her conception, by a singular grace and privilege of Almighty God . . . [Mary] was preserved immaculate from all stain of original sin' (Henry Denzinger, *The Sources of Catholic Dogma*, trans. Roy Deferrari (St Louis: Herder Books, 1955), p. 50). By this is meant that Mary was conceived naturally but at the moment when soul and body fused, God intervened, giving her a soul untainted by sin. *Cf. Con. Church*, 59.

[2] Papal ratification of this belief came in November, 1950. 'By the authority of our Lord Jesus Christ, of the blessed Apostle Peter and Paul, and Our own authority, We pronounce, declare and define that the dogma was revealed by God, that the immaculate Mother of God, the ever Virgin Mary, after completing her course of life upon earth, was assumed into the glory of Heaven both in body and soul . . .' (Denzinger, p. 648). *Cf. Con. Church*, 59.

[3] *Con. Church*, 56.

it decay at death (assumption). Through her co-operative response to God's grace she became Mother of God and the New
Eve.

Mary's unique relationship to God has usually led theologians
to ascribe to her a threefold role in human life. First, she has
been described as *Coredemptrix*, cooperating with Christ in the
work of saving men.[4] This idea is also present in the Council
documents, though the word itself does not appear. As Divine
Mother, 'Mary is united with her Son, the Redeemer, and
with His singular graces and offices'.[5] After her ascension 'she
did not lay aside this saving role'.[6] The second role is that of
Mediatrix, dispensing Christ's grace to needy sinners.[7] This
title is used by the Council, and Mary is also said to be
'mother to us in the order of grace'.[8] Third, she is said to be
the Queen of Heaven who rules with God in providence.[9]
Vatican II applied this same title to her[1] and evidently believed
that she was providentially ruling the Council itself. In his

[4] Although this has not been promulgated as an official article of faith,
several popes have made reference to it. In 1918, for example, Benedict XV
declared that Mary offered Christ up at Calvary and so 'with Christ she
redeemed the human race' (Denzinger, p. 502). The actual word *Coredemptrix*
first appeared in 1913 in the encyclical *Sunt Quos Amo* when the faithful were
urged to add the name of Mary to that of her Son in their prayers.
[5] *Con. Church*, 63.
[6] *Ibid.*, 62.
[7] In 1891, Leo XIII said that 'just as no one can approach the highest
Father except through his Mother', so she is 'the Mediatrix to the Mediator'
(Denzinger, p. 488). The feast of Our Lady, *Mediatrix* of All Graces is
celebrated on 31 May. During Mass, the following prayer is said: 'Lord
Jesus Christ, our Mediator with the Father, who didst deign to make thy
blessed virgin Mother our own mother also, and *Mediatrix* between thyself
and us, graciously grant that whoever comes before thee to ask thy bounty
may be gladdened by obtaining all he asks through her.'
[8] *Con. Church*, 62, 61.
[9] Pius XII in his encyclical *Ad Caeli Reginam* declared that 'from this divine
maternity it is easily deduced that she too is Queen, since she brought forth
a Son who, at the very moment that He was conceived was ... King and
Lord of all creatures. As a result, St John Damascene could rightly and
deservedly write these words, "Truly she has become the Lady Ruler of every
creature since she is the mother of the Creator".'
[1] *Con. Church*, 59.

opening speech, Pope John prayed that Mary would 'dispose all things for a happy and propitious outcome'.[2] It was only proper that John should conclude his speech in this way for he had begun it by placing the whole Council 'under the auspices of the virgin Mother of God'.[3]

Whether we are thinking of Mary's experience of grace (with the corollaries of immaculate conception, sinlessness, perpetual virginity and assumption) or of her roles in human life (as *Coredemptrix*, *Mediatrix* and Queen), the foundational verses of Scripture about her are Genesis 3:15 and Luke 1:28. Consequently, the Council's handling of these two verses is disappointing. No doubt there are many who hoped that the rekindling of interest in biblical exegesis among Roman Catholic scholars would lead to a revision of the way these verses have been traditionally interpreted.

Genesis 3:15 contains the promise of God to the serpent that 'he shall bruise your head, and you shall bruise his heel'. The Douay-Rheims version translates '*she* shall crush' for 'he shall bruise' and '*her* heel' for '*his* heel'. The reference is then assumed to be prophetic of Mary's birth.[4] Vatican II also understood it to be so. This is such a significant manipulation of the text that some justification is to be expected. Accordingly, the Douay-Rheims version gives this explanation: '*She shall crush*; So divers of the fathers read this place conformably to the Latin. . . .' The Latin referred to is probably that of the Vulgate, a Latin translation of the Hebrew completed early in the fifth century AD. It is important to note, however, that the Hebrew itself simply states that *he* (*hū'*) would crush the serpent. The Septuagint, the Greek translation of the Old Testament probably begun in the middle of the third century BC, correctly renders this as *he*, using the masculine pronouns *autos* and *autou*. This early testimony confirms the view that the original

[2] Abbott, p. 719.
[3] *Ibid.*, p. 710.
[4] This alleged conjoining of Mary and Christ in the work of redemption means that 'from eternity', 'Mary is connected with Her Son in the providence of God' (Burke, p. 70).

intention of the passage was to speak of one of Eve's descend-
ants in particular who would be masculine and would also be
the object of the serpent's attack.

The Roman change from 'he' to 'she' had been made at
least by the fifth century AD. At this time Jerome observed that
when the angelic greeting of Luke 1:28 is converted into Latin
('*Ave Maria*') and the '*Ave*' is then spelled backwards, one has
the Latin word for Eve ('*Eva*'). Others then argued that it was
not illegitimate to conclude that, on this basis, Mary must have
been the second Eve, in whom the promise of Genesis 3:15 was
realized. She crushed the serpent's head.

There are four reasons for rejecting this. First, there is no
textual support for it. Kittel's *Biblia Hebraica* offers no textual
variant which would allow us to substitute 'she' for 'he'.
Second, there are no exegetical grounds for this change. The
words of Genesis 3:15 were addressed to Eve and the promise
was that her masculine seed would conquer Satan. Translating
'he' as 'she' is quite illegitimate. Third, there are serious
theological objections to the concept of the second Eve. For
one thing, it is Adam rather than Eve who is regarded as
representing mankind. For another, Scripture speaks of the
last Adam but never of the second Eve. To be the last Adam,
Christ had to represent the vast company of Christian people
in the same way Adam had represented mankind (Rom.
5:12–21; 1 Cor. 15:45–50). In Christ's case, representation
and salvation were involved in one another. To speak of Mary
as the second Eve is to imply that she too has saved mankind.
The Council did not hesitate to say this,[5] but in the process it
lost touch with the teaching of Scripture. Finally, there is a
serious methodological flaw in the argument. We have no right
to change the teaching of Scripture to read 'conformably to
the Latin' of later centuries. It would be far better if the
Council had either rejected the biblical testimony outright or

---

[5] In several places the Council protests that its doctrine of Mary in no way
detracts from the unique work of Christ. But it is difficult to see how this
can be.

rejected its own traditions. As it is, Catholics still believe that Scripture sanctions devotion to Mary.

The second verse which is thought to support Marian dogma is Luke 1:28. The angel Gabriel came to Mary and said, 'Hail O favoured one, the Lord is with you!' The crucial word here is the one translated *favoured*. On this word, Catholics have built their view of Mary's unique experience of grace with all the implications and corollaries which follow. According to Arndt and Gingrich, the word means 'to bestow favour upon, favour highly'. In Ephesians 1:6, which is the only other use of this word in the New Testament, it is used of all Christians who have experienced the forgiving grace which God 'freely bestowed on us in the Beloved'. If we can deduce from Luke 1:28 that Mary was conceived without sin, lived without it and was assumed into heaven, can we not also deduce from Ephesians 1:6 that all Christians have similarly been conceived without sin, live without it and will rise from the grave shortly after being buried? But, of course, this is ridiculous. The Bible teaches that we are conceived in sin (Ps. 51:5; Rom. 3:23), and Mary was not exempt. If Mary herself needed to be saved from her sins, she could not possibly join with Christ as *Coredemptrix* to save man.

In a sharp critique of the Council's teaching on Mary, Philip Edgcumbe Hughes has this to say:

Despite all qualifying clauses, the effect, in both logic and practice, of the Mariology of the Roman church is to rob Christ of the uniqueness of his redemptive and mediatorial office. How can it be otherwise, when Christ declares that it is he who gives life to the world (John 6:33), whereas the Council, without disputing this, affirms that Mary 'gave Life to the world' (DV II, 86); when the apostles consistently declare that the likeness to which we are to be conformed is that of Christ (Rom. 8:29; II Cor. 3:18; Phil. 3:21; I John 3:2), whereas the Council affirms that Mary 'is the Church's model' and that those who 'strive to increase in holiness . . . raise their eyes to Mary who shines forth to the whole community of the elect as a model of virtues' (DV II, 86, 93); when the Scriptures consistently declare that Christ alone was without sin (II Cor. 5:21; Heb. 4:15; 7:26; I Pet. 1:19; 2:22; I John 3:5), whereas the

Council affirms Mary was 'entirely holy and free from all stain of
sin' . . . and when the New Testament consistently declares that
Christ is the sole and unique Mediator between God and man and
the only Redeemer of our race (I Tim. 2:5; Heb. 9:15; John 14:6;
Acts 4:12; I John 2:1), whereas the Council . . . applies the title of
'Mediatrix' to Mary and affirms that by her 'cooperating in the
work of human salvation' there was a 'union of the Mother with
the Son in the work of salvation' (DV II, 84).[6]

Despite the biblical testimony against Marian devotion, it
is still fostered, not merely by peasants, but preeminently by
popes and the Church's most sophisticated theologians. Why?
Karl Barth may have the answer although his judgment
sounds harsh:

In the doctrine and worship of Mary there is disclosed the one
heresy of the Roman Catholic Church which explains all the rest.
The 'mother of God' of Roman Catholic Marian dogma is quite
simply the principle, type and essence of the human creature
co-operating servantlike (*ministerialiter*) in its own redemption on
the basis of prevenient grace. . . . [7]

Mary is the prototype of the Roman Catholic. By her
cooperative action, she won the approval of God. By implication, does not this divine approval also extend to the whole
Catholic Church? And is not the basis of works in salvation
also divinely approved? In Mary we have seemingly irrefut-
able validation of Roman theology at its fundamental points.
If God be for Rome, who can be against her?

If, from a Catholic perspective, Marian doctrine must be
preserved in order to retain the integrity of Catholic theology
as a whole, then from a Protestant perspective, it must be
reformed if the New Catholicism, which says that it is concerned
only with what Scripture teaches, is to be believed. The fact
that Vatican II changed so much else but left this doctrine
intact is not insignificant. Is the New Catholicism really willing

[6] Philip Edgcumbe Hughes, 'The Council and Mary', *Christianity Today*, 12,
8 December 1967, p. 10.
[7] Karl Barth, *Church Dogmatics*, trans. G. T. Thomson, *et al.*, I (Edinburgh:
T. and T. Clark, 1936), 2, 143.

to allow its teachings to fall under the scrutiny of the biblical Word or is it, too, reading Scripture only when and where it is convenient to do so? 'Nothing less than the Gospel of our redemption is at stake here,' comments Hughes. 'Today the challenge comes afresh to us and to our Roman Catholic friends to "hold fast the profession of our faith without wavering". The Gospel forbids us to acknowledge any mediator . . . other than our Saviour Christ, who alone is the Way, the Truth, and the Life.'[8] Will we stand together in this affirmation?

[8] Hughes, p. 10.

ANNOTATED BIBLIOGRAPHY

This bibliography is mainly intended for theological students and pastors to use as a guide to a firsthand acquaintance with the New Catholicism. It is by no means comprehensive; rather, it merely suggests which books should be consulted first. Since the basic rule in research of this kind is first to consider primary sources, this essay begins with the texts and speeches from the Council. When these are mastered, secondary source comment and criticism should be read and then, if the student so desires, the work of the new theologians can be tackled. It is important to observe this order. Leaders in the New Catholicism must be studied against the background of the Council. Without this context, the real significance of their work will be lost.

1. Council Documents

In 1966, the Vatican published the approved texts in a handsome volume entitled *Sacrosanctum Oecumenicum Concilium Vaticanum II: Constitutiones, Decreta, Declarationes* (Romae: Libreria Editrice Vaticana, 1966). It is, of course, all in Latin, and this may seem a discouraging start to a bibliography. But even for the student with no knowledge of Latin, it is still very useful. It contains an index which is far more comprehensive than any that have appeared in English translations. With the use of a good dictionary, all the references can be drawn up on any word, theme or doctrine in the conciliar documents. Failing this, a student wanting to pursue a theme will probably have to use either Raymond B. Fullam's *Exploring Vatican II* (New York: Alba House, 1969), which has arranged the important passages thematically, or A. Hasting's *A Concise Guide to the*

Documents of the Second Vatican Council (London: Darton, Longman and Todd, 1968). On the text itself, the best English translation is by Walter Abbott, ed., *Documents of Vatican II* (London: Geoffrey Chapman, 1967).

Speeches which were delivered on the Council floor and which were influential on the formation of the texts can be found in the volume edited by Yves Congar, Hans Küng and Daniel O'Hanlon entitled *Council Speeches of Vatican II* (London: Sheed and Ward, 1964).

The preparatory reports drawn up by Pope John's committees prior to the Council have now appeared in English as *Preparatory Reports: Second Vatican Council* (Philadelphia: Westminster, 1965). A comparison of these reports with the finished and approved texts is often revealing.

2. *Commentaries*

Protestants will find it difficult to interpret the Council documents without assistance. This is due partly to the subtleties of the Latin language, partly to the delicate ambiguities in the texts and partly to the almost esoteric nature of Catholic theological language. All of the individual constitutions, decrees and declarations have excited a considerable number of commentaries. There are, in fact, too many to mention. Included here are two commentaries which cover all the documents.

For established or potential scholars, the three-volume addition to *Lexikon für Theologie und Kirche* deserves to be mentioned. It is entitled *Das Zweite Vatikanische Konzil. Konstitutionen, Dekrete und Erklärungen* (Freiburg: Herder, 1967–68). It is also available in English in the five-volume set edited by Herbert Vorgrimler entitled *Commentary on the Documents of Vatican II* (London: Burns and Oates, 1967–69). This is a very thorough piece of work, written by many of the leading Catholic theologians. As it happens, the majority are 'progressive' in their stance, so the student should beware of bias. An interesting and often incisive analysis also emerged from an international theological conference held at the University of Notre Dame in Indiana. Edited by John H. Miller, it is entitled *Vatican II: An Interfaith Appraisal* (Notre Dame: University of Notre Dame Press, 1966). This contains the work of Protestants as well as Catholics.

3. Council History and Theology

It is impossible to separate the theology of the documents from what took place in the Council. Often the significance of a passage becomes plain only when the conflict which took place over it is known. The history of the text really provides the key to its theological significance.

Quite the most readable and informative account of the Council are the four volumes by Xavier Rynne entitled *Letters from Vatican City* (New York: Farrar, Straus, 1963), *The Second Session* (New York: Farrar, Straus, and London: Faber, 1964), *The Third Session* (New York: Farrar, Straus, Giroux, 1965), *The Fourth Session* (New York: Farrar, Straus, Giroux, 1966). Later, Rynne put out a single-volume summary of these called *Vatican Council II* (New York: Farrar, Straus, Giroux, 1968). Xavier Rynne, by the way, is a pseudonym used for self-protection. It would appear that he feared retaliation from the conservatives whom he has mercilessly berated and sometimes maligned in these books. The student should realize that these volumes are part of an ideological war and thus contain propaganda along with their history. Despite this, however, they deserve first mention. Other accounts worth consulting are Henri Daniel-Rops, *The Second Vatican Council: The Story Behind the Ecumenical Council of Pope John XXIII* (New York: Hawthorn Books, 1962); the four volumes by D. Horton, *Vatican Diary* (Toronto: United Church Press, 1962–65); and *Council Daybook* (Washington: National Catholic Welfare Conference, 1965). If the student has time to spare, he might also like to view the pictures in L. Wolleh and E. Schmitz's *Council: A Documentation in Pictures and Text of the Second Vatican Council* (Toronto: Macmillan, 1966).

On the theological side, undoubtedly the most lucid presentation is B. C. Butler's *The Theology of Vatican II* (London: Darton, Longman and Todd, 1967). The book began life as the Sarum Lectures at Oxford which Butler, one of the most 'progressive' of English Catholics, was invited to deliver. The book is highly readable and informative although it is critical of traditional ideas. Most of the leading Catholic theologians have had something to say on Vatican II, so it is difficult to be selective beyond this. But perhaps the following books deserve some mention. First there is J. Ratzinger's *Theological Highlights of Vatican II* (New York: Paulist Press, 1966). This account is not as comprehensive as Butler's nor is it quite as candid. One has the impression Ratzinger cannot quite bring himself to say what is really on his mind. Then, there is the work of K. Rahner who has written extensively on some aspects of the Council's teaching. His book, *The Church After the Council* (New York: Herder and Herder, 1966), for example, tries to draw out its over-all theological significance though this study is not, strictly speaking, on the theology of the Council. Küng also has discussed many of the aspects of conciliar theology as, for instance, in his *Council in Action* (New York: Sheed and Ward, 1963). Edward Schillebeeckx has two little paperbacks on the subject entitled *Vatican II: The Real Achievement* (London: Sheed and Ward, 1967) and *Vatican II: A Struggle of Minds and other Essays* (Dublin: Gill and Son, 1963). Considering his stature as a theologian, these are disappointing productions. A book of no mean interest is Maritain's *The Peasant of the Garonne* (London: Chapman, 1968). Whereas all the books mentioned previously in this section have been sympathetic to the new thinking, Maritain's is decidedly critical. It is not specifically an attack on the Council's theology; rather, it is a broadside against the new mentality in Catholic thought. These theologians, he contends, are 'kneeling before the world'.

On the Protestant side, the book deserving prime consideration is G. C. Berkouwer's *The Second Vatican Council and the New Catholicism* (Grand Rapids: Eerdmans, 1965). This happens to be the only substantial production to have come from within traditional Protestantism, and it also appears to be among the best productions on this subject. Berkouwer, more than anyone else, has perceived the underground movements which led to Vatican II. The material in the book is organized in an unusual way, but this is something of a hallmark of Berkouwer's writing. His work on the Second Vatican Council is considerably more irenic than his earlier one entitled *The Conflict with Rome* (Philadelphia: Presbyterian and Reformed Publishing Co., 1950).

Two books of interest in this category are Karl Barth's *Ad Limina Apostolorum* (Edinburgh: St Andrew's Press, 1969) and Oscar Cullmann's *Vatican II: The New Direction* (New York: Harper and Row, 1968). These books are of interest mainly because of their authors. Barth, after all, has carved out his role in contemporary theology as a fierce critic of Rome, but in this particular book he is surprisingly mild. One of the better books to emerge since the Council is E. Schlink's *After the Council* (Philadelphia: Fortress Press, 1968). It is more penetrating than, say, George Lindbeck's *The Future of Roman Catholic Theology* (London: SPCK, 1970), which is, in other respects, a comparable volume.

Finally, a book dealing with the key figures in the Council, the churchmen who have continued to make an impact, is Walter Abbott's *Twelve Council Fathers* (New York: Macmillan, 1963).

4. Reference Works

On the Council itself the *Dictionary of the Council*, edited by J. Deretz and A. Nocent (London: Chapman, 1968), is invaluable for checking details and dates. On the latest Catholic thinking, Karl Rahner has edited a useful six-volume tool entitled *Sacramentum Mundi: An Encyclopedia of Theology* (London: Search Press, 1968–70). Its companion set, representing the new Catholic approach to an understanding of Scripture, is edited by J. Bauer and entitled *Sacramentum Verbi:*

An Encyclopedia of Biblical Theology (New York: Herder and Herder, 1970).

If the student needs to range more widely and perhaps check matters antecedent to the Council, the following tools should be used: *New Catholic Encyclopedia* (New York: McGraw-Hill, 1967), a magnificent multi-volume set representing the most recent scholarship on almost every conceivable religious subject; L. Bouyer's *Dictionary of Theology* (New York: Desclee, 1965); P. Parente *et al.*, *Dictionary of Dogmatic Theology* (Milwaukee: Bruce Publishing Co., 1951); and G. Podhradsky's *New Dictionary of the Liturgy* (London: Chapman, 1967).

5. Contemporary Developments

There is obviously no way of keeping abreast of current thinking other than by reading the new books and journal articles as they appear. However, two aids which should not be overlooked are *Concilium* and *The Pope Speaks*. The former, which is really a journal, though it also appears in book form, began life in the Council. Undoubtedly some of the most innovative and creative writing to emerge from the progressive Catholic wing has appeared in its pages. It covers a wide range of subjects, giving the student a good opportunity to feel the progressive pulse at most points. The second is also a journal, and it offers some of the papal speeches and documents in English translation. This gives an English-speaking student direct access to some of the Pope's teaching otherwise closeted away in the official Vatican journal, *Acta Apostolicae Sedis*, or the Vatican newspaper, *L'Osservatore Romano*.

6. Bibliographies

For further study, students will find some help in two published bibliographies, one of which is pre-Vatican II and the other on Vatican II. Elmer O'Brien edited the first, entitled *Theology in Transition: A Bibliographical Evaluation of the 'Decisive Decade' 1954–1964* (New York: Herder and Herder, 1955). This is a fairly useful collection of bibliographical essays on the biblical,

patristic and liturgical studies in this period. The second book
was compiled by Charles Dollen and is entitled *Vatican II:
A Bibliography* (Metuchen, N. J.: Scarecrow Press, 1969).
Unlike O'Brien's book, this is not a critical evaluation of the
literature. Rather, Dollen has simply sought to list everything
which has been written in English on Vatican II. He has
gathered both books and articles and, since the latter are easily
overlooked, this is a useful tool.

INDEX